365
WAYS TO BEAT
STRESS

EDITED BY
ADAM GORDON

365

WAYS TO BEAT

STRESS

HOW TO RELAX & FIND PERFECT CALM

WATKINS
Sharing Wisdom Since 1893

365 Ways to Beat Stress
General Editor: Watkins Media Ltd

First published as *1001 Ways to Relax* in the United Kingdom and
Ireland in 2002.
This revised edition published in 2019 by
Watkins, an imprint of Watkins Media Limited
Unit 11, Shepperton House
89–93 Shepperton Road
London N1 3DF

enquiries@watkinspublishing.com

British Library Cataloguing-in-Publication Data:
A CIP record for this book is available from the British Library

ISBN: 978-1-78678-214-4

10 9 8 7 6 5 4 3 2 1

Typeset in Cera Pro and Cardenio Modern
Printed and bound in China

CONTENTS

INTRODUCTION

Just as it takes all kinds of people to make our world so various and so beautiful, so too it takes many forms of relaxation to create rest and renewal at each level of our being and in each area of our lives.

I have to confess that when we first set out to think about *365 Ways to Beat Stress*, the thought occurred to me, "This is absurd, there's no way there are 365 ways to engage with stress." However, it wasn't long before I realized there are probably tens of thousands of ways. And all of these methods differ from each other in time, place and depth – by which I mean that there is a vast difference between, on the one hand, relaxing for a few minutes in order to free ourselves from the physical and mental tensions that we accumulate in the average day; and, on the other hand, years of practising the deepest forms of spiritual relaxation, in the manner recommended by the sages and the saints. And there is an equally huge gap between relaxation that relieves a few stressful symptoms and ways that reach deep inside the soul and heal the core causes of our spiritual discomforts.

During the process of creating and gathering material for this compendium of tools, tips and techniques, I have been reminded time and time again how the simplest of changes at the level of our thoughts, perceptions and actions can release us from our anxieties. I believe that what makes this little book a special companion is that it truly contains remedies, rescues and exercises for almost every commonplace situation and any moment of our waking lives. From the home to the workplace, from early morning to late evening, from our relationships with others to our very important relationship with ourselves, you will find literally hundreds of ideas to experiment with.

Many years of researching stress and helping others to understand, manage and prevent this totally curable condition have brought home to us here at Watkins the overwhelming fact that everyone has different needs at different times. That's why, in this mini-compendium, you'll find methods that address the tensions in your body, techniques to deal with sadness, guilt and other disturbing emotions, visualizations to help you transform old patterns of negative thinking, and meditations to give you access to the deepest dimensions of spirit. For it is, of course, deep in the soul that we will always find the most natural and eternal calm.

There are many ways to use this little book. You could spend a week or two working through a specific section, trying out the most relevant techniques and noting down others to experiment with some time in the future. You could focus on one area of your life that is not as relaxed as you would like it to be, and you could work with the contents pages to find specific ways to help you change. Alternatively, you could dip in and out, and enjoy the delights of serendipity as you give yourself the gift of a new way to relax every day. And if you decide to do one of the most relaxing things in life, which is to give a gift to a friend, then why not become what you might call a "benevolent adviser" by pointing out to the person who will be fortunate enough to receive this book from you the three numbered exercises that you recommend they read first, simply because you sense that this is what would help them most.

Don't be fooled by the obvious simplicity of some of the suggestions. You may be surprised to discover how the smallest of actions can trigger the greatest rewards. And don't miss one of the underlying threads of the book: the reminder that ultimately "being" comes before "doing" in the lexicon of relaxation. True, everything you do will have an effect on your state of being; but more importantly, when you learn to create your state of being, when you can establish peace in your heart, invoke love in your relationships and donate happiness to everyone around you, then you will know that your spirit is as relaxed and as joyful as it can ever be.

We live in tense, turbulent and, for many people,

unrelaxing times – of that reality there is no doubt. But we can easily avoid adding to the turbulence. In fact, we can become one of those people for whom the world has a great need: those who can stay calm in a crisis, cool in the midst of chaos, and focused on the positive when all around are inclined to reinforce the negative. If we can stay relaxed and calm, this helps others to do the same. If we can always respond with a positive note, we help others stay in tune with the symphony of life. If we can keep seeing life through optimistic eyes, we can brighten someone else's day in a single second! In all these ways we do much more than maintain a calm state of being within ourselves: we radiate outward an extremely positive energy, and in so doing we serve the world.

Mornings

WAKING WELL

001. **WAKE UP NATURALLY,** without an alarm clock, at least once a week if you can. This will help you reconnect with your bodily cycles (or circadian rhythms, to use the scientific term). Note that going to bed an hour earlier will not necessarily bring forward your natural waking time by an hour – you may find that you lie awake, worrying that you can't sleep. If your circadian rhythms make you a night owl at heart, go with the flow and have a weekend lie-in when you need one. If you're a lark, spring out of bed when the time seems right – you may find there's time before breakfast to do some worthwhile meditation.

002. **DRAW INSIGHTS FROM DREAMS** in the morning while they are still fresh. We cannot confirm the truth of dream symbolism, as the unconscious runs no helpline. But if, in a spirit of adventure, we start to explore possible meanings of dreams, we can usually arrive intuitively at constructive insights, which heighten self-awareness and feed into our subsequent tranquillity.

003. **IMMEDIATELY ON WAKING,** "think how you can give joy to at least one person today." These are the words of the nineteenth-century philosopher Friedrich Nietzsche – a surprising person to have come up with such an uplifting thought, as he is more often associated with deeply sceptical, angst-ridden philosophy.

004. **ENJOY THE SYMPHONY OF NOISE** that penetrates your bedroom – the traffic outside, the birdsong, the jackhammers, the news on your neighbour's radio. Don't let extraneous noises stress you, just because you aren't in control of them. Instead, imagine that all these sounds are a wonderful random concert for which you have a privileged free ticket. Listen mindfully. Enjoy each cacophonous moment.

005. **ENGAGE ALL FIVE SENSES** each morning, as soon as you awaken. The sight of sunlight, the sound of birdsong, the feel of a towel, the taste of fruit juice, the smell of toast – check off each sense in turn as the brain-signals flood in.

STARTING THE DAY

006. **THROW OPEN A WINDOW** to start the day with deep drafts of air and blow away the cobwebs that have settled on your well-rested spirit in the night. Even if you've had a window part-way open all night, this is a good way to get the air circulating freely. Don't let bad weather put you off – rain or snow can be just as refreshing for the spirit as brilliant sunshine.

007. **CLOSE YOUR EYES** for a whole minute, and imagine you were born without the gift of sight. Open your eyes and let the world flood your senses. Then imagine your "higher senses" opening to bring you an intense experience of all the world's beauty. After your imaginary act of sense deprivation you will no doubt feel a corresponding gratitude. Try to keep a sense of that gratitude with you as the effect of your minute's darkness fades.

008. **MEDITATE ON YOUR BREATH** immediately after getting out of bed. As you breathe in, keep your chest still and push out your abdomen – as if you were blowing up a balloon in your stomach. As you breathe out, drop your shoulders and imagine yourself squeezing out air, as though pressing water out of a sponge. Do this for ten complete breaths. As you do so, feel the energy of the new day enter your body.

009. **WATCH A SPIDER SPINNING ITS WEB.** Treat the web like a mandala (a sacred diagram used in meditation). Focus on the intricate concentric pattern as it develops. As you appreciate its complexity and beauty, be aware of the web's dual existence – out there in the world as well as an impression in your mind. Allow the image to hang in your perception, just as the web itself hangs in empty space.

010. **IMAGINE SIX IMPOSSIBLE THINGS BEFORE BREAKFAST,** like the White Queen in Lewis Carroll's surreal fable, *Alice's Adventures in Wonderland*. This activity primes the mind to expect the unexpected, and deal with it in a calm, accepting manner. To get you in the mood, here are two examples: a country where clockmakers are arrested for mistreating time; a reclusive hermit who believes that he can love his fellow men and women more purely and intensely from an uninhabited island.

011. **SING IN THE SHOWER.** Singing has its roots in the innate happiness of the spirit, reminding us of our true nature. It is also a celebration of the interfusion between body, mind and soul. As you sing, allow the vibration to begin in your heart, fill your body and then the room – it's good to be alive!

012. **PUT ON A BRIGHT SHIRT** and add a splash of colour to your day. Your very presence will liven up the environment for those around you! Each colour has a symbolic significance. Pick one that resonates particularly with your mood or your goals that day: red is associated with courage and passion; yellow with sunlight and optimism; blue with openness, calm and spiritual peace. If a conservative dress code operates in your workplace, remember that there's nothing to stop you wearing a brightly coloured tie or necklace instead.

BREAKFAST

013. **HAVE A SMOOTHIE** for breakfast. Pulped in a blender rather than juiced in a juicer or citrus press, smoothies provide a more filling, slower-releasing alternative to juices. This is because, unlike juices, smoothies contain fibre, which slows digestion and the absorption of nutrients, as well as mobilizing the gut.

014. **LIMIT YOURSELF TO ONE COFFEE** in the morning – if you can't break the habit entirely. Consumed in excess, coffee over-stimulates the adrenal glands, leaving you irritable and nervy, and causes dehydration by acting as a diuretic. Experiment with caffeine-free coffee substitutes, such as chicory, dandelion and Californian coffeeberry. If you can't find these ready-prepared in the stores, make your own with the roots of chicory or dandelion, or the seeds of Californian coffeeberry. In each case, let the roots or seeds dry before roasting, grinding and then percolating them like ordinary coffee grounds.

015. ALWAYS EAT BREAKFAST. The traditional wisdom
of enjoying a breakfast fit for a king and reducing
the size of subsequent meals throughout the day,
culminating in a pauper's dinner, is well judged. A
generous breakfast kick-starts your metabolism, sets
you up for the day, and replaces lost fuel after the
night's "fast".

016. ENJOY A PORRIDGE BREAKFAST. Oats provide a
sustainable source of energy to get a winter's day
off to a good start and are also rich in B vitamins,
which help to keep you calm. For a summery
alternative to porridge, try Bircher muesli – packed
with nutrients, this was the original muesli recipe,
concocted by Dr Bircher for the patients at his
clinic in the Swiss mountains. Soak a handful of oats
in water or unsweetened fruit juice overnight (to
render them more digestible). Combine the soaked
oats with one grated apple, a handful of chopped
dried or fresh fruits, a handful of chopped nuts or
seeds, and two tablespoonfuls of natural yogurt
or sweetened condensed milk.

LOOKING AHEAD

017. **FORGET YESTERDAY'S MISTAKES.** Today is a new day, your mind has been refreshed by sleep, and there is no need to believe that yesterday's misjudgements or misfortunes will repeat themselves. Make yourself a checklist of all that you have learned from past mistakes – and now move on.

018. **IMAGINE A ROBBER** has visited you in the night and made off with all your past experiences and ingrained habits, but you have a magic spell that brings back everything you assent to. You are, for the moment, free of any burden you choose not to accept. Today, whatever happens, you have the awareness to select an appropriate response, rather than reacting automatically. See what it feels like – for a while – to be the person you wish to be.

019. DECIDE TO BE HAPPY today, no matter what happens or who does what. It is within your power to make this leap. Happiness is the true condition of the self-aware, and its source lies within ourselves. To decide to be happy is a positive, self-fulfilling action, comparable to "I do" in a marriage ceremony.

020. CREATE A PERSONAL AFFIRMATION and declare it twenty times to yourself each morning. Affirmations are simple, positive "I am..." statements (such as "I am at peace," "I am a tower of strength") that build self-esteem and a strong sense of self. They counter the negative messages that we often give ourselves by reminding us of our intrinsic value. In your affirmation include those qualities that you readily recognize in yourself, as well as those you are prospecting for. If you are having difficulty recognizing your strengths, ask a friend what positive qualities they see in you. Include these in your affirmation. Create specific affirmations to prepare you for days that you know will be particularly challenging. Cover the qualities that will be most helpful to you when coping with the day's events.

021. **PLAN FOR ANY DIFFICULT SITUATIONS** that the day is likely to hold. Think of the qualities you expect to need – for example, focus and concentration for an intellectual task, tact and diplomacy for difficult people, an attitude of acceptance for potential disappointments. Decide whether you're likely to need more of any quality than you'll be able to summon naturally and impromptu. If so, plan to allow time before the event to collect yourself and meditate into existence the required qualities from your innermost reserves.

022. **CALL YOURSELF FROM HOME** before setting off for work in the morning and leave a message on your work voicemail – perhaps a reminder to yourself of some treasured insight, a resolution for the day ahead, or perhaps even a joke to drive away morning blues. Do this for someone else – perhaps a friend or family member who is not enjoying their work at the moment – to sound a positive note as soon as they arrive at the workplace.

OFF TO WORK

023. **TRANSFORM YOUR JOURNEY TO WORK** into quality time with yourself by using the opportunity for reading, listening to music or low-key meditation. (If you travel by public transport, you may need to leave home earlier, to be sure of a seat.)

024. **WALK THE PRETTY ROUTE** to work if there is one – if this necessitates a detour, bear in mind that the exercise is good for you.

025. **CLOSE YOUR EYES** and think of the crowds as a communion of souls enjoying the shared experience of travel. Feel the warmth of humanity around you. Rejoice in the contact.

026. **DO A SARDINE MEDITATION** in a crowded train. You are surrounded by strangers. Imagine that you are all sardines, packed together in one small tin. Rather than resenting those around you, you recognize that essentially you are all alike in nature and share the same predicament. This will give you a sense of fellow-feeling with all the other commuters.

027. **GIVE UP YOUR SEAT** to someone who needs it more than you. You will be surprised how good this simple act of kindness makes you feel.

028. **WALK MINDFULLY TO YOUR WORKPLACE,** noticing what is going on around you. This will give you accurate local knowledge, and you may make some useful discoveries. In particular, check out the local cafés and look for new establishments opening up where one day you might choose to meet a friend or hold an informal business meeting.

Dealing with Stress and Emotions

QUICK FIXES

029. **VISUALIZE A BLUE BUBBLE** stretching protectively around your body. Blue is associated with protection and tranquillity. Imagining ourselves enveloped in this blue film helps to prevent our energies from being leached by those around us. This technique is particularly useful when we feel stressed by crowds. Alternatively, draw a circle of protection around yourself. Imagine a circle being drawn around you on the floor or ground, then imagine invisible, impregnable but totally transparent walls rising from the circle to protect you. You are invulnerable: nothing can touch the essential self whose dominion is the invisible tube you have placed around yourself.

030. **7/11 BREATHING** is a simple technique for dealing with the sharp, shallow breaths resulting from an agitated mental state. Breathe in slowly and steadily to the count of seven; then breathe out slowly and steadily to the count of eleven. Continue with this rhythm of in-breaths and out-breaths until your breathing becomes more relaxed and regular and the tension that triggered your anxiety begins to subside.

031. **SQUEEZE A STONE IN YOUR HAND** as hard as you can; then gradually release your fist. Rock the stone gently as if making peace with it. Do this every time you feel stressed or angry, until the feelings drain away.

032. **BE PAVLOVIAN.** The Russian scientist Ivan Pavlov discovered that the body can be trained to react on cue whenever a particular stimulus is given. Try exploiting this effect to induce a sense of inner calm during moments of stress. First you need to put Pavlov's principles into practice. Whenever you are feeling happy and relaxed, recall an event in your life that gave you pleasure, and at the same time pinch one of your earlobes. If you do this often enough, you will unconsciously come to associate earlobe pinching with the physiological state of relaxation. This technique equips you with a means to combat the physical symptoms of stress: in theory, when you pinch your earlobe, your stress levels should diminish automatically, as your brain remembers its training.

033. **TRY STRESS BALLOONING.** Imagine loading your worries into the basket of a hot-air balloon. In your mind's eye, untie the ropes that hold down the balloon and watch it rise. Your problems become more remote as the balloon disappears into the clouds.

034. **BREATHE OUT A NEGATIVE, BREATHE IN A POSITIVE.** This exercise involves placing a particular imaginative interpretation upon your breathing. Sit comfortably and allow your body to relax. Now focus your attention on your breath. As you breathe out, visualize the negative emotion, such as anger, streaming out of your nostrils; as you breathe in, imagine an appropriate emotion, such as compassion, being drawn into your lungs and from there into your bloodstream, where it is carried to every part of your body. Continue this exercise, exhaling anger and inhaling compassion, for about five minutes.

035. **DON'T JUST DO SOMETHING, SIT THERE!** Contrary to the usual exhortation, this is sometimes the best approach when emotions are running high, your problems seem insurmountable, or your intuitive compass is not giving you a clear direction to follow. Simply take a few moments to sit in stillness, gathering your strength. Give your mind and body permission to relax.

036. **RECALL A SMILE** on the face of someone who loves you, to give you the strength to deal with problems. (If you find it difficult to picture their face clearly, you might find it easier to visualize a photograph of them instead.) Respond with a smile of your own and watch the smile of your loved one broaden further.

DIFFICULT CHOICES

037. TAKE A STEP, ANY STEP. Paralysis can set in when we spend too long agonizing over what to do next. The key is to take an action and listen for any positive or negative feedback – remembering that the absence of feedback is itself feedback. You can then use this information to adjust your course if necessary.

038. ASK YOURSELF what the "youthful sage" within you would do whenever you have difficulty making a choice. The youthful sage is your childhood self – as children we tend to be more in touch with our intuition. When we grow older, many of us feel that this innate wisdom becomes stifled by conditioning and experience. Consulting your childhood self is a way of reconnecting with your intuition, helping you to make a choice consistent with your true self.

039. **READ A CLASSIC NOVEL** – a diversion that is particularly useful when you find yourself obsessively analysing a problem without reaching any solutions. The linear narrative structure of a traditional novel can help to shift your circular thoughts into more progressive patterns, subliminally priming you to move through your problems toward possible solutions.

040. **SOLVE IT BY WALKING.** This is a translation of a Latin proverb, *Solvitur ambulando*. Take a half-hour walk and allow yourself to be soothed by the rhythm of your steps. You may detect an "inner sieve" at work, bringing your lightest, happiest thoughts to the surface, allowing your heaviest thoughts to drop away.

041. **ROUTINE CHORES,** such as cooking and cleaning, or repetitive activities, such as driving, knitting and sewing, are particularly helpful in loosening the grip of recurring thought patterns, because they engage the left-brain, leaving the right-brain free to pursue alternative, more creative thoughts.

042. **SIT ON IT.** If a problem doesn't have to be resolved immediately, it can sometimes help to sit on it for a while. Make a note in your diary to reconsider the problem at a later date. Put it to sleep until then and get on with other things. After a week or so you may find that the problem has solved itself or that your mind is clearer and more able to find a resolution.

043. **WRITE YOUR WORRIES DOWN.** This simple action can reduce your attachments to your worries, putting them into perspective and freeing you to think about other things. If you can't let them go, take time out to address your worries. Find a peaceful spot where you are unlikely to be interrupted and write down your anxieties. What is the worst that can happen? What is the best possible outcome? Decide on some actions you can take over the next few days to reduce the likelihood of a negative result.

044. **DON'T TRY TO RESOLVE EVERYTHING IN A DAY.** Make a list of outstanding worries in the early evening, then just switch off and enjoy yourself for the remainder of the day. Difficult tasks are much better faced with fresh energy in the morning.

045. **FOLLOW YOUR INTUITION** when trying to decide whether a particular course of action is right or wrong. If you feel logic overruling your intuition, close your eyes and imagine the optimum course of action as a ball of light rising from your stomach and filling your mind with truth.

BREAKTHROUGHS

046. **VISUALIZE A LOCKED BOX** sitting on a table in front of you. You have the only key. Inside the box is an object which represents the solution to a current problem. Close your eyes, remind yourself of the problem, then see yourself opening the casket. What lies inside? What clues does it give you?

047. **MAKE A PATH THROUGH A DENSE JUNGLE** in your mind when faced with seemingly impossible situations. This visualization will strengthen your belief in yourself and your capabilities, as well as your faith that a way will be found. Imagine you are sitting on the ground surrounded by impenetrable thickets, a cacophony of animal noises all around. From your place on the ground, you visualize a path opening up behind you. When the moment comes for you to stand up and turn around, there is the path exactly as you imagined it. As you walk forward, you leave the noise behind. You can feel the trees watching you, smiling at you, celebrating your courage.

048. SEE THE LIGHT AT THE END OF THE TUNNEL.

When problems seem hard to bear, this meditation
will give you hope of better things to come. Close
your eyes and imagine yourself in total darkness.
After a few minutes, visualize a spot of light in the
distance. As you walk toward it, the spot grows
gradually larger. Eventually the outlines of a tunnel
become visible. Sunlight floods in, revealing the
floor and walls of the tunnel. Beyond the entrance
you see a verdant landscape. Step out into the
sunlight and feel the warmth on your skin. Feel a
sense of peace as you find yourself in the world
once more.

049. CROSS A BRIDGE from problem to solution. In
your mind, visualize the vivid embodiment of your
problem situated on the bank of a river. Now begin
to construct a bridge across the river to reach the
other side. The bridge has five piers, each of which
represents a quality that you will bring to the
situation: identify these qualities. Now see yourself
walking across the bridge. On reaching the other
side, you discover an object. This represents a
solution. What does it look like? What does
it mean?

$050.$ **THE RULE OF THREE.** One way to be more thorough in what we do is to break down our actions into three phases. For example, if you want to forgive someone, there would be the genuine wish to forgive; the act of forgiveness itself (whether silent or spoken); then the follow-through. Try this one–two–three approach when you want to deal systematically with an issue.

$051.$ **BLITZ YOUR PHOBIAS** by gradual acclimatization. This involves exposing yourself to the object or situation that you fear at increasing levels of intensity. Progress to the next level only occurs when comfort is achieved at the current level. For example, if you had arachnophobia (fear of spiders), you would begin by looking at a photo of a spider. When you felt comfortable with this you would look at a model spider, then a real spider several feet away, then a spider closer up... and so on.

052. **TAKE A GLOBAL PERSPECTIVE** on your problems to understand their true scale. Imagine that you are orbiting the Earth in a flying saucer. Satellites beam images on to your console screen from anywhere you choose: office workers streaming ant-like through the streets of New York; a fishing fleet off the coast of Iceland; dolphins diving playfully in the Atlantic; wild geese flying in formation across the desert plains of Africa. As you zoom in close to watch the activities of these creatures you become aware that each one forms an integral part of the web of life. Consider your problems in the context of this greater whole. Do they seem smaller by comparison? Perhaps easier to bear?

053. **DON'T BE A CATASTROPHIZER.** When forecasting events, there is often a temptation to fixate on worst-case scenarios in the name of being prepared. However, this approach usually causes unnecessary angst – things are rarely as bad as we expect. In such situations, take sensible precautions, but make it a rule not to preoccupy yourself with fears of imagined future disasters.

054. **DECOUPLE YOUR WORRIES.** When worries are lumped together they can seem so overwhelming that your entire life becomes one big insurmountable problem. Instead, try separating out your worries so that you can deal with each one individually. When you do this, each worry seems smaller and as a result easier to understand and ultimately deal with.

055. RETUNE YOUR MEMORIES. Look back over any memories from the past that continue to cause you emotional pain. Examine your story of what happened. Try to separate the factual events from your interpretation. Is there a more positive way that you can interpret these events? You may find that retelling the story from a different, more positive angle loosens the emotional hold of your original version.

056. IMAGINE YOURSELF IN A YEAR'S TIME. Ask yourself how important the feelings you have now will seem to you then. This is a particularly good way to deal with anger, but it can also work for other emotions such as jealousy and resentment. Remember that in reality problems seldom have the immutable shape in which we might imagine them.

057. **THINK OF REASONS WHY YOU CAN** do something rather than why you can't – all it takes is a shift in your attitude. Once you have broken the negative logic of your thinking, you gain space in which positive approaches can incubate.

058. **TAKE THE OPTIMISTIC APPROACH.** According to psychological research, optimists adopt a specific "explanatory style" when interpreting the events that happen to them, attributing positive events to their own abilities and seeing negative events as isolated instances of bad luck. This approach bolsters self-esteem and peace of mind, giving those who practise it greater resilience and an ability to cope with difficult situations.

AKING CHARGE

059. **ACCEPT NEGATIVITY.** Often we compound negative states of emotion by getting frustrated with ourselves for not being as calm and centred as we would like, which in turn only makes us feel worse. Rather than trying to beat yourself into a positive frame of mind, take the time to acknowledge exactly how you are feeling. See if you can find a neutral place within yourself to sit side by side with your emotions, without trying to push them away. You may find that this loving acceptance of your own feelings works as an antidote, tempering some of the pain.

060. **TAKE RESPONSIBILITY FOR YOUR EMOTIONS.** Blaming others for "making" you feel a certain way leads to "victim consciousness". Remember, you have the freedom to choose how you react to the world around you. To believe otherwise is to give away your personal power.

061. **RELEASE THE WORRY ANIMAL.** Sometimes worry is a monkey, jumping around your mind, filling your life with anxiety. Sometimes it is an elephant, which stands in front of you – a huge obstacle that obscures your vision. Identify an animal that best symbolizes your worry and then set it free by opening the doors of its cage (our worries are held captive by our minds). See it walk, run, fly or swim away.

062. **WRITE A LETTER FROM YOUR CALM SELF** to your worried self if you feel in need of advice and reassurance but there's no one at hand to provide it. Be as practical as you can. You may surprise yourself how easily you can tap into the calm voice inside.

063. **CHALLENGE YOUR INNER CRITIC.** Many of us possess a critical inner voice that chips away at our self-esteem, undermining all our achievements, laughing at our mistakes. For every error or failing that you catch your critic berating you for, think of two positive qualities that outweigh it.

064. **DECLARE AN AMNESTY FOR NEGATIVE THOUGHTS.** Whenever you have one, imagine that it's come to give itself up. Accept its surrender and send it on its way, taking care not to criticize it for existing in the first place.

065. **QUESTION THE WORD "SHOULD".** Used about yourself, this word reflects pressures that you are allowing to influence your behaviour. Take a moment to become aware of these pressures: do you wish to give them governance over what you do? Used of others, the word "should" can denote a subtle attempt at control. Find a replacement before the word reaches your lips.

066. **BANISH "HAVE TO".** The phrase "I have to" implies a surrender of will to an outside force. Empower yourself by taking responsibility for your actions. Replace the words "I have to" with "I choose to". You always have a choice, however difficult it may be. Notice how this subtle shift in attitude affects your perception of what you are choosing to do.

TIME OUT

067. **RETREAT TO THE GREEN ROOM.** In most television studios there is a place called the "green room". This is a quiet room in which actors can take time out from the glare of the spotlights on set. If you find yourself in a difficult situation, imagine that you are an actor on a television set. When the stress becomes unbearable, take advantage of your actor's privileges and head for the green room. In this quiet mental space, you can clear your mind of all thoughts for a while. Once you've regained your composure, return to the set and resume work.

068. **READ TO A CHILD** a story of their own choosing. Whether the book offers soothing tales of the antics of furry animals or an action-packed adventure story, it will transport both you and the child to another realm, away from the troubles of everyday life. Any lingering traces of negative emotion will soon be washed away by the child's innocent pleasure.

069. **THE SHIP OF PEACE.** Imagine you have a free day and you are standing in a port on the quayside. The ship of peace sails in from the sea to collect you. Once on board you see the gentle smiles on others' faces, feel the peaceful atmosphere everywhere on the ship. A whistle blows and the ship sets sail. Visualize the peaceful sights you come across on your voyage.

070. **VISUALIZE A SCENE OF NATURAL CALM.** It may include a lake set against a spectacular backdrop of mountains, or perhaps a cluster of tall palm trees, rustling gently in a warm tropical breeze – whatever holds most meaning for you. Enjoy the feeling of peace this scene gives you. Choose one object from the scene, and whenever your inner calm is disturbed, summon this object to mind. It will evoke your scene of tranquillity and all its associated feelings.

071. **THE COUNTRY CALLED RELAXATION** is very different from home. Imagine yourself arriving there. What would you see on disembarking from the plane and making your way through the capital to your hotel? How does everyone manage to be so relaxed in all they do? What attitudes or habits might make this possible for you? Now come home for a vacation. Bring the culture of this newly discovered country with you.

072. **PLAN A TRIP TO AN EXOTIC PLACE** – you do not actually have to go there. Taking a mental journey to an unknown place is an escape from your daily routine and an invitation to the mind to go beyond the mundane. Research details about your chosen destination. Visualize the journey. What will it be like when you arrive? What are the best sights on and off the beaten track?

073. **IMMERSE YOURSELF IN A DIFFERENT CULTURE.** For example, read about the Japanese way of celebrating a wedding, or the mysterious ways of the native American shamans.

TRAVEL STRESS

074. **LEAVE A PAPER TRAIL.** Before embarking on your travels, leave photocopies of your passport, tickets, insurance details and travel cheques with family or friends. If your documents get lost or stolen, you will be able to get at the necessary information with minimum disruption to your trip.

075. **GO TO BED AT THE LOCAL TIME** when you arrive at your destination. During long-haul flights it is common to cross several time zones in a short space of time. Time differences, combined with cramped and dehydrating conditions on the flight, can lead to symptoms of jet lag upon arrival. These include extreme fatigue and poor concentration. Adjusting to the local time as soon as possible helps to counteract these debilitating symptoms. (This is easier when flying west than east.)

076. **PERFORM LEG EXERCISES** during flights to ward off DVT (deep vein thrombosis). DVT occurs when a (potentially fatal) blood clot forms in the body. During the enforced inertia of flights, leg exercises help to encourage the free flow of blood through the limbs. Every half an hour, rotate and flex your ankles and squeeze your leg muscles twenty times. Every hour or so, get up from your seat and stretch your legs.

077. **BANISH BOREDOM** by refusing to fight it. Treat the time you have at your disposal as a luxury – a welcome opportunity to exercise your imagination.

078. **BE A HERO OF TIME.** If you are delayed during your journey, think of waiting as a challenge to your inner strength – but one that you can vanquish without difficulty. As you sit or stand there, feel yourself growing in stature with every minute that you wait. Enjoy the quality of time as it passes: see it as an invisible heroic frieze that celebrates your conquest of boredom.

079. **PERFORM SHOULDER ROLLS** at traffic lights, moving your shoulders up, back, down and around in a continuous movement to reduce neck and shoulder tension. Repeat ten times. Similarly, practise chin tucks while driving. Looking straight ahead, tuck in your chin (pretend that you're trying to give yourself a double chin while moving your head back toward the head rest). This exercise will help to lessen neck strain and prevent you from slouching forward.

080. **RECONSIDER YOUR ATTITUDE** toward other drivers. Are you impatient, pressing right up behind the car in front to pressure them to go faster? Are you overly competitive, overtaking other cars for the sake of it? If so, take a deep breath and focus your attention on the purpose of your journey – namely, reaching your destination without endangering yourself or others.

Positive Change

THINKING POSITIVE

081. **RUN THROUGH THE ABCD OF CHANGE:** A is for Awareness of what you need to change. B is for Belief in your ability to change. C is for Commitment to the idea of change. D is for Discipline and your willingness to stick to your plan of change.

082. **REAWAKEN YOUR CHOICES.** We tend to forget that we have choices at many levels. We can choose the direction of our lives, the thoughts and reactions that we have, even the feelings we create. Cultivating awareness of how we are creating our current experiences – of what we're doing and why we're doing it – gives us the freedom to create different experiences by making alternative choices.

083. **SEE LIFE AS A JOURNEY,** not a destination. Destination consciousness (a constant preoccupation with future goals) ensnares us in anxieties related to time as we fret about our progress. By contrast, journey consciousness (an openness to the present moment) enables us to appreciate the delights and lessons that greet us at every twist and turn along the way.

084. BAN SELF-DENYING PHRASES such as "I can't" or "I don't do things like that" from your vocabulary: they tend to become self-fulfilling prophecies by their very utterance. Similarly, ban habitual expressions of procrastination, such as "I'll start tomorrow", and phrases of displaced initiative, such as "Is there a plan?" Our choice of words tends to reflect our thinking. If we are able to change what we say after becoming aware of the phrases we use, it becomes possible to change what we think and ultimately what we do.

085. ACT "AS IF". Our minds are very suggestible. If you act as if you are serene, happy and free of stress, eventually you may find that it becomes a reality.

086. **SWITCH ON THE LIGHT.** Feeling down without knowing why is a common experience. In such moments we may let out a silent cry for help – forgetting sometimes that we can help ourselves. If you find yourself in this position, imagine that you are in a dark room. The room is your life and the darkness your mood of gloom. Now reach out and switch on the light. Amazingly the room is filled with reasons to be cheerful. On a pad of paper, write or draw everything that you see. Carry this record around with you to provide yourself with a ready source of inspiration.

087. **APPRECIATE LAST YEAR'S GIFTS.** Although New Year's resolutions are useful for setting the course for the following year, they can imply flaws and failings in the past. For a truly positive start to the New Year it's important to find value in the one that's just ended. Reflect on the experiences that you found most challenging and think of three positive outcomes for each one that you can carry forward into the next year – perhaps lessons you have learned, wonderful people you have met, inner strengths you have discovered.

088. **MATCH YOUR VALUES AND GOALS** in order to feel fulfilled in what you do. If there's a gap between the two, you will experience either tension or apathy. High values plus empty goals equals no motivation to reach your targets. Low values plus ambitious goals equals no real satisfaction in your achievements. Ask yourself which are more positive: your values or your goals? Make any necessary adjustments to either in order to bring the two factors into line with each other, thereby correcting any inner disharmony.

089. **LOOK AT THE BIG AND SMALL.** Think about the subjects to which you pay most attention: which of them have become too dominant in your life? Now consider areas you may be neglecting. Awareness of imbalances of this kind often provides sufficient motivation to effect a redistribution of energies.

090. **DO MORE OF WHAT YOU'RE GOOD AT.** It's almost certain to be something you enjoy and, as a bonus, this will strengthen your self-confidence.

091. **TRY SOMETHING NEW** at least once a month – whether it's reading a classic children's book, joining a tango class, or riding pillion on a motorbike. Exposing yourself to unfamiliar experiences stretches your mental and physical horizons, acclimatizing you to change and loosening the grip of routine.

092. **ADMIT WHEN YOU DON'T KNOW.** In today's world we are constantly under pressure to have answers to and opinions about everything. Such pressures may make us painfully conscious of the gaps in our knowledge, whether in politics, economics, history, the arts or any other field. However, there is no need to feel guilty or embarrassed about what you don't know. Refuse to join the ranks of those who claim to be an instant expert on topics of popular interest. Nobody can know something about everything. Accept your blind spots, and don't be stressed about them.

093. **ADMIT YOU WERE WRONG** when you know, deep down, that you were. This instantly frees you from the tension created by sustaining the illusion that you were right!

094. **GIVE UP ON YOUR BOOK** if you're not enjoying it. Find one that does please you. You owe no obligation to any writer.

TIME AND MONEY

095. TREAT TIME AS A CONVENIENCE, not an obstacle. Time is merely nature's way of preventing everything from happening at once. Think of it as a robotic helper, programmed to remain in the background until it's required – for example, when you are meeting a friend in a restaurant.

096. DO LESS, EXPERIENCE MORE. In our fast-paced modern world, there is a constant pressure to do more in less time. Consequently, there is little time to appreciate what we are doing, to enjoy the experience of being alive. One way to ease this situation is to schedule in some time for yourself. To do this you may need to reduce the number of commitments you take on. With less to do you will have more time to reflect on and appreciate your experiences.

097. **CONSIDER DOWN-SIZING.** A more drastic step, for those who are comfortable in money but poor in time, is to work shorter hours for less pay. This could involve a shift from full-time to part-time employment, taking a step down the career ladder, or even a complete change in career. Think seriously about it: many people find it immeasurably enriching.

098. **HAVE AN EXPENSE-FREE DAY.** With a little forward planning this should be possible, even on a work day (for example, you may need to prepare a packed lunch to take into the office). See how many you can have in a week. It's a great way of saving.

099. **BE MINDFUL OF MONEY** – in other words, ask yourself what money means to you. Try to concentrate on its practical rather than its symbolic value. Don't allow a connection to take root between money and self-esteem. Your true assets are your personal values, not your monetary valuation. Even when money is elusive, you have the power to thrive, as a loving, peaceful being.

100. **CREATE A MONEY MAGNET.** Whenever small change clutters up your purse or wallet, empty it into a jar. Over time the money will accumulate until you have a significant amount. Change the coins for notes at a bank and spend the money on a treat for yourself, or donate it to a charitable cause.

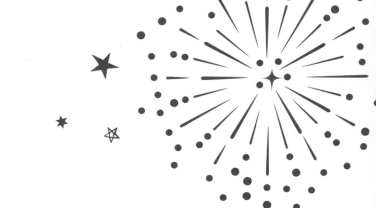

LONG-TERM CHANGES

101. **MAKE A LIFE-PLAN.** Write a list of ten things that you want to happen in your life, from places you want to visit to events you want to bring about. Tick them off as you achieve them. With each tick you'll feel a sense of fulfilling your own destiny.

102. **SNAPSHOT YOUR GOALS.** One reason that many of us lack concrete goals is that we don't have a clear picture of them. Imagine that your mind is a camera. Now create detailed mental images of your goals in your life's key areas – career, family, relationships, personal growth. One by one press the button to open the shutter and imprint your goals on your mind.

103. **LOOK WHERE YOU'RE GOING** – rather than focusing on the obstacles that lie in your way. The obstacles may be imaginary, but even if they're real, you won't get far if you allow them to dominate your whole field of vision.

104. MAKE A MOTOR OF CHANGE.

Assemble a patchwork of inspiring words and images. Leaf through old magazines, cutting out any passages or pictures that represent your goals or aspirations. Stick them onto a sheet of cardboard to form a collage. Pin this to your kitchen noticeboard as an encouragement to take steps toward your dreams.

105. TAKE BABY STEPS.

Often the best way to progress toward a goal is to take one small action each day that brings your dreams closer to fruition. For example, you might spend a lunchtime gathering information on the internet, write an email requesting a brochure, or make a phone call to someone who can help you.

106. FIND A ROLE MODEL.

Look for someone who has achieved the kind of goals that you are aiming for. See what you can find out about the steps they took and the strategies they used to arrive at their current position. Perhaps you could write to them or give them a phone call asking for their advice. Alternatively, if they are in the public eye, you might come across informative interviews with them or books about their lives.

107. NEVER STOP LEARNING –

about yourself, other people, and the world at large. Learning ensures that we remain flexible and responsive, able to deal with whatever happens to us and make the changes that we seek.

Mind and Spirit

MEDITATIONS AND VISUALIZATIONS

108. **DEVELOP YOUR MEDITATION POSTURE.** In order to relax during meditation it is important to sit comfortably. The traditional position for practising meditation is the lotus posture (sitting with both legs crossed, the tops of the feet resting on the opposite thighs). Easier versions are the half-lotus (sitting, one foot resting on the opposite thigh), or simply sitting upright on the floor with the legs crossed. If you feel any pain in your knees in these positions, place a cushion under your pelvis. Alternatively, sit on an upright chair with your legs uncrossed. Sit forward on the seat so that your back isn't resting on the back of the chair.

109. **MEDITATE LIGHT-HEARTEDLY.** If you find it hard to relax and free your thoughts during meditation, it may be because you are tense or anxious. Before you start your session, think of something funny – humour is profoundly liberating to the spirit.

110. **MUSE ON A PARADOX.** The Greek philosopher Empedocles once said: "God is a circle whose centre is everywhere and whose circumference is nowhere." Such conundrums defy rational understanding, hinting at truths deeper than words can express. To appreciate their meaning we must allow them to hang in our minds without seeking logical explanations.

111. **CONTEMPLATE DUALITY.** Taking a coin, look first at the side bearing a head. As if seeing through the head, visualize an image of the obverse side of the coin. Then turn the coin and do the same with the other side. In the two-sided coin we find a symbol of duality, a reminder of the multi-faceted nature of reality. There is always more than one way of looking at things.

112. **DRILL TO THE CORE** in your meditations, as though drilling for oil. You will need patience as you work through different layers of your psyche to reach the core of consciousness. Imagine the drill-head of your focused attention slicing through your accumulated layers of experiences, memories, perceptions, beliefs, until finally you break through to pure love, pure peace, pure contentment at the centre of your being.

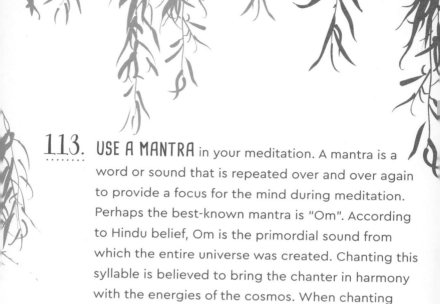

113. **USE A MANTRA** in your meditation. A mantra is a word or sound that is repeated over and over again to provide a focus for the mind during meditation. Perhaps the best-known mantra is "Om". According to Hindu belief, Om is the primordial sound from which the entire universe was created. Chanting this syllable is believed to bring the chanter in harmony with the energies of the cosmos. When chanting Om, sound the final consonant for about four seconds, so that it becomes a hum. You could also chant an appropriate word, such as "calm", where again you can linger on the final "m".

114. **DISSOLVE YOUR BODY** in a visualization. Lie comfortably on your back. Starting at the toes and working toward your head, imagine your body turning to liquid as you tense, then relax, each part in turn. Finish by relaxing the mind, concentrating deeply, then letting your thoughts dissolve and float away.

115. **VISUALIZE A WIND** blowing straight through you as you stand against it. As it whistles through your body, imagine it unpicking the threads of every negative thought and feeling that has ever been woven into the fabric of your being.

116. **BECOME THE SKY.** Visualize the vast blue sky above. Be aware that it is without limits, without boundaries, embracing the world. Consider that our minds, and therefore our whole selves too, are without limits or boundaries. As the sky fills your mind, experience the boundlessness of self and spirit – infinitely rich, infinitely calm. Do not strain to capture infinity – just relax in acceptance of the boundless sky inside and outside your boundless consciousness.

SPIRITUALITY

117. **DEVELOP A SPIRITUAL PRACTICE.** Any activity that serves to centre you, bringing you a sense of deep inner connection with both yourself and the world around you, can form the basis for a spiritual practice. Examples include Eastern disciplines, such as yoga and meditation, as well as various aspects of Buddhism and Zen, such as the spiritual pilgrimage and the tea ceremony (see point 201, page 109). The activity will absorb you completely, so that you reach a state of "flow" whereby you are one with what you are doing. Practise this as regularly as possible – it will give you a point of steadiness in your life.

118. **LEARN FROM SPIRITUAL TEACHERS,** such as the Buddha or St Augustine. Study their lives and teachings and follow their precepts in small but important ways. Ask yourself whether they would approve of actions you are contemplating.

119. MEET YOUR ANGEL. Close your eyes and imagine yourself at the edge of a dark forest. Ahead of you is a path. You follow the path, which winds deep into the heart of the forest. Eventually you come to a clearing where there is a temple. A bright white light is emanating from the doorway. As you enter the temple, you see that the brightness is in fact a beautiful angel – a being of light. The angel holds out its arms and you embrace. In that moment of connection you realize that your angel knows and understands everything about you and your life. It is your companion on your journey and will always be there for you to offer unconditional love and support. Whenever you feel lost or alone, simply return to this sacred place within yourself and your angel will be there to greet you.

120. **CALL ON YOUR SPIRIT GUIDES.** Whether you understand them as the embodiment of your inner spiritual wisdom, or as all-knowing celestial beings akin to guardian angels, your spirit guides can be of help whenever you are faced with a difficult situation, or have a question that you are unable to answer. Just think, speak or write your question. You will receive the answer through one of a number of different routes – for example, in a dream, during a conversation with someone, or in a book that you are given, recommended or impelled to buy. Simply pay heed to the signs all around you.

121. **FOLLOW THE TAO.** Tao is a Chinese word meaning "the way" or "the path". Taoism is an Eastern philosophy based on the principle that life involves a ceaseless movement and flow from one form to another. Problems arise when we attempt to resist or control the natural pattern of change. Harmony can be restored by following the Tao – that is, by "going with the flow", accepting the ever-changing pattern of life without judgement or resistance.

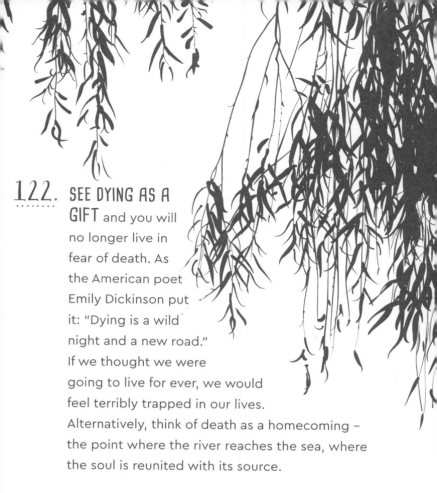

122. **SEE DYING AS A GIFT** and you will no longer live in fear of death. As the American poet Emily Dickinson put it: "Dying is a wild night and a new road." If we thought we were going to live for ever, we would feel terribly trapped in our lives. Alternatively, think of death as a homecoming – the point where the river reaches the sea, where the soul is reunited with its source.

123. **VISIT A GRAVEYARD.** The peaceful atmosphere of most graveyards makes them ideal places for quiet reflection. Read the epitaphs. Feel a sense of oneness with life's eternal rhythms.

WISHES, PRAYERS AND RITUALS

124. **CREATE A PERSONAL ALTAR** in a quiet corner of your home – ideally in a private room, such as a bedroom or study. Cover a small table or box with a cloth and decorate it with items that represent your sources of inspiration and strength. These could include photographs of family and friends, flowers and stones symbolizing the natural world, and so on. Meditate or pray in front of your altar. Feel its beneficial energies.

125. **DISCOVER THE POWER OF PRAYER.** Everyone can benefit from prayer, whether religious or not. In prayer we express our hopes and dreams, as well as acknowledging our blessings. In so doing we both affirm our direction in life, and draw upon the strengths that we need to continue our journey. Your prayer can take whatever form you choose. Address it to your source of wisdom and strength: this could be your higher self, the universe, or the divine as you understand it.

126. **DROP A COIN IN A WISHING WELL** or fountain and make a wish for good things to happen to a friend, or even an enemy, as you throw the coin into the water. A benevolent heart is always more content than one that is merely concerned with itself.

127. **MAKE A WISHING TREE.** Wishing trees originate from a Celtic tradition which involves tying coloured scraps of clothing, called "clouties", to a tree and making a wish. To make your own wishing tree, find an old item of clothing that you are ready to part with. After ripping the clothing into shreds, find a suitable tree and tie one of the pieces of cloth onto it, making a wish or creating a goal as you do so. Repeat this until your tree is hung with all your life goals. Through this ritual you release the weight of the past and allow your vision to invoke your future.

128. **USE A BALLOON** as a messenger for your wishes. Having formulated a wish, write it on a piece of paper and tie it to a helium-filled balloon. Take the balloon outside and release it to the skies. Watch the balloon diminish to a vivid speck as it carries your wish out into the ether. Taking positive action in this way will encourage you to work toward realizing your desire and perhaps prompt destiny to respond by supporting you. As your thoughts create a reality, performing this action in your imagination can be equally powerful, provided that you take time to envisage all the steps in detail.

129. **PURGE YOUR FEARS** with a ritual burning. Write them on a piece of paper, and either throw the paper into the flames of a fire or light it with a candle and dispose of it safely. Make this affirmation: "My fear is within my control. I banish it to oblivion."

ELF AND WORLD

130. **RECONNECT WITH THE ELEMENTS.** Whenever you find yourself distracted or agitated, unable to remain present in a given situation, use the elements to ground yourself and regain a natural perspective. For example, you could walk barefoot outside; sit or lie on the ground; let sand or pebbles run through your fingers; surround yourself with candles; swim or float in a lake; even lean into a high wind, allowing the air to support you. If it's inconvenient to perform any of these activities, practise the elements meditation instead. According to Eastern traditions, the entire physical universe is made up of the five elements – fire, water, air, earth and ether. Meditate on the unique qualities of each of these elements; and end with a prayer of thanks for firemen, sailors, pilots and miners who grapple with the four main elements for our benefit.

131. **LIE ON THE GROUND AND GAZE AT THE SKY.** From this perspective we can appreciate the true vastness of the sky as it arches above us, holding both the Earth and ourselves in its supportive embrace. We become more deeply aware of our intrinsic connection with the cosmos, the small but vital role we play in the order of nature.

132. LISTEN TO THE RAIN. The insistent rhythm of raindrops bouncing off a roof or onto a backyard can have a lulling effect. During the day, appreciate the rain's ability to block out less welcome sounds; at night, relish the snugness of being warm and dry in bed as the rain falls.

133. **A DOUBLE RAINBOW** is an extraordinary phenomenon. See it as a reminder of the uniqueness of your life and a blessing on all you do. Relish the experience and be thankful for the privilege of this auspicious signal from nature.

134. **WALK IN THE RAIN** without an umbrella when it's warm outside. Take pleasure in the water droplets as they hit your body, trickling in cool rivulets over your skin. Enjoy the feeling of intimacy with the elements – it is a reminder of our connection with the natural world.

135. **FLOAT IN A POOL, LAKE OR SEA.** Stretch out your arms and legs, surrendering all attempts to control your movement. Just lie there, enjoying both weightlessness and "will-lessness". Imagine all your roles in life, and all your worries, rising off you like steam. You are pure self, pure mind, pure spirit.

ACCEPTANCE

136. **TRUST IN LIFE'S FLOW.** If you find that you are struggling to achieve a desired result in any situation, it could be that you are trying to force the issue. Instead, sit back and accept whatever happens. That which is rightly yours will come to you. Nothing takes place before its designated time.

137. **ACCEPT CHANGE.** Nothing stays the same for ever. True relaxation comes not from controlling life's flow, but from allowing yourself to be carried along by the flow without fear of the future or nostalgia for the past.

138. **MEDITATE ON BIRD MIGRATION** in order to reconcile yourself to change. Year in, year out, birds experience the seasonal upheavals of migration. However, these global movements are not seen as disruptive: they are simply a manifestation of the ebb and flow of nature's cycles. In the same way, understand the changes in your life as part of a broader pattern of cyclical change instead of obstacles on a linear trail.

139. **VISUALIZE A WEEK-OLD SPARROW** holding tight onto a branch. Its first flight is just moments away. The chick looks up as its mother glides past, inviting it to take to the air. In accord with its natural impulses, the chick lets go of the branch. Down toward the earth it plunges at first, until suddenly, flapping its wings, it recovers, finding the strength and skill to rise and soar. The bird gives a heartfelt squawk of gleeful achievement – its rite of passage successfully completed. Hidden within this visualization is a simple message: let go of your branch. Detachment brings freedom, which in turn brings happiness.

140. **LET GO OF LOST OPPORTUNITIES.** There will always be opportunities in your life that you didn't take, because you didn't see them, because you were already committed, or because you valued something else more highly. Rather than cursing yourself for missing these opportunities, remember that you made the best choices you could at the time. Look ahead and follow your chosen path, seeking the doorways that are open to you and forgetting about those you have closed.

141. **SAY THE SERENITY PRAYER:** "God grant me Serenity to accept the things I cannot change, Courage to change the things I can, and Wisdom to know the difference."

THE SIMPLE LIFE

142. **BE LIGHT.** To be light is different from being trivial, flippant or uncaring. Lightness is a graceful ability to dance triumphantly in the face of destiny – an approach to life that contrasts with the slow, lumbering weight of solemnity. Try to cultivate lightness for a while, but don't labour the point. Allow it to come to you as naturally as leaves to a tree.

143. **JUST BE GOOD.** We don't need an opportunity to do good in order to be good! All doing begins with being. Being is doing to an enlightened soul. Being good means being positive when others choose to be negative, being open when others choose to be closed, being accepting when others opt for resistance. Goodness is a state of being – and it is stressless!

144. **STOP AT ENOUGH.** "Do more", "achieve more", "acquire more" are the most mischievous mantras of the modern world. They represent a constant drive toward more than enough, creating a never-ending spiral of unfulfilled promise. Reject them, and be satisfied with all your assets and your endless potential.

145. **RATION YOUR EVENINGS OUT** to two or three evenings a week. By limiting your number of social engagements, you will appreciate them much more. Use your free evenings to pursue other interests, such as exercise, reading or creativity, and to recharge your batteries and your bank balance.

146. **BE A TRUSTEE, NOT AN OWNER,** of your possessions. This subtle shift in perception frees you from fear of loss or damage.

147. **USE PEN AND PAPER,** the old-fashioned way, instead of using your computer. This links your words more directly with your thoughts, connects you with an honourable tradition, and gives your eyes and posture a break from the tyrannical screen. Handwrite letters to friends and family – it's much more personal than typing letters or emailing, and will be greatly appreciated by the recipient.

148. **AVOID NEWS OVERLOAD.** Many of us bury our heads in newspapers and news magazines, because we feel a responsibility to keep up with current events. However, in a world of global communications the brain can't absorb all the news available to us. To avoid overload, select carefully what you want to read. Instead of trying to keep up with all world events, specialize in two or three topics and follow them in depth.

149. **MARK LANDMARK NEWS EVENTS** in your diary. This will help you to see your own life in a broader historical perspective, giving you a sense of proportion about your experiences.

150. **GO ON A MINI-RETREAT** for just one day, or for a morning or afternoon. Ban the phone, the television and radio, and the car (unless you need the car to transport you to your chosen place of tranquillity). Meditate and give thanks for your blessings. Mindfully appreciate your time spent alone.

WONDERFUL YOU

151. **BE KIND TO YOURSELF.** As the Buddha wisely said, "If your compassion does not include yourself, it is incomplete." Be aware of the judgements that you cast upon yourself and gently seek to dismantle them.

152. **REFLECT LOVINGLY ON YOURSELF.** Imagine that you are sitting quietly by a still pool surrounded by palm trees and rocks. As you look down into the still water, you see your face reflected there. Notice the calmness in your expression. As you gaze into your reflected eyes, you are struck by their serenity, their infinite capacity to love. Your reflection is content in your presence, and always happy to respond to your summons whenever you gaze into a mirror-like surface. It admires you. Return its esteem. Offer love to your own image.

153. **SHOWER YOURSELF WITH GOOD WISHES.** Visualize yourself strolling through a dense jungle, then arriving at a pool into which a waterfall is flowing. Stand beneath the cascade of water, imagining that the spray is saturated with the blessings and good wishes of all the people in your life today. Resolve to say a silent thank you with your eyes next time you see them.

154. **IMAGINE YOU'VE BEEN KIDNAPPED** by the conspirators in a plot to eliminate all pain: they are truth, love and humour. Gazing steadfastly into your eyes, Truth reminds you that life is an adventure and should not be taken too seriously. Arms round your shoulders, Love shyly ventures that your spirit is dazzling. Then Humour shows up to tell your all-time favourite joke. You laugh again, as you have a thousand times before. Your laughter echoes around the world; all pain is vanquished.

155. **DEVELOP A PERSONAL SUCCESS CHART.** Draw up a chart showing the months of the year across the top and the different areas of your life down the side – relationships, work, creativity, personal development, health. At the end of each month, reflect on the successes that you have had in each area. This could be anything from completing a project at work to attending a regular dance class. For each achievement place a gold star in the relevant column to reward you for your efforts. You could also create for yourself a life chart to remind you of the achievements in your life thus far.

156. **ENJOY BEING YOUR AGE.** You'll never be so young again! Appreciate your growing wisdom and experience – it would sit oddly with a younger body and face. Remember, you can feel young, and therefore be young, by remaining ever-curious about the world, open to new challenges and experiences.

157. **CELEBRATE WRINKLES,** grey hairs and other small signs of ageing. They reflect maturity. Wear them proudly – they are the badges of your wisdom and experience.

158. **SPEAK UP FOR YOUR BELIEFS,** however unpopular you feel they may be. It's good to get into the habit of small-scale risk-taking: it's essential to our growth and our ability to handle difficult situations. On the other side of risk is the quiet satisfaction that we have defeated our biggest enemy – our fear!

159. **VALUE THE POWER OF THOUGHT.** Reflect on the formidable creative powers of nature – caterpillars transforming into butterflies, new buds forming on a pruned tree. See your own ideas in a similar light: you have an infinite capacity to spin one idea out of another. You are the emperor of the world of thought.

Body

TOUCH

160. **DISCOVER THE BENEFITS OF MASSAGE.** Scientific studies have shown that massage is one of the easiest ways to attain and maintain good health. On a physical level, massage increases the circulation, relaxes the muscles, aids digestion and stimulates the lymphatic system, thereby aiding elimination of waste from the body. On an emotional level, massage relaxes us and creates a sense of love, warmth and security.

161. **EXERCISE YOUR HANDS** before massaging yourself or another to increase their flexibility and sensitivity. Start by vigorously rubbing the back of your left hand with the palm of the right. Repeat with the hands reversed. Then, rub your palms together until they feel hot. Finish by holding your palms together, then lifting your elbows up until your palms no longer touch. Press your fingers against each other and hold for six seconds, stretching the finger and wrist joints.

162. **MASSAGE WITH ESSENTIAL OILS.** Use a light vegetable oil, such as almond, grapeseed or soya, as a carrier for the essential oils, which are extremely concentrated. Dilute one to three drops of essential oil with a teaspoon of carrier oil. Using essential oils will help your hands glide smoothly over the skin, as well as bringing both giver and receiver the benefits of the essential oil. For a basic massage oil, try lavender, which eases stress, relieving symptoms such as headaches, insomnia, nervous anxiety and mild depression.

163. **MASSAGE YOUR FACE.** Stress makes us unwittingly knot our brows or clench our jaws. Use your index and middle fingers to iron out these tensions. Start by making circles on your brow, moving from the middle toward your temples. Then make sharp upward strokes along the bridge of your nose. Finally, close your eyes and gently rest the heels of your hands in your eye sockets. Do each of these three stages for about a minute.

164. **EASE A HEADACHE** or migraine by applying gentle pressure with the forefingers to the acupressure points that lie around the eyes. There are seven of these: one between the two eyebrows in the middle of the brow; two in the middle of the eyebrows; two below these, halfway along the lower ridges of the eye sockets; two in the slight indentations at the outer edges of the eye sockets, next to the temples. For each point in turn, hold the pressure for three seconds and then gently release.

165. **RELEASE TENSION** in your scalp. Grasp your hair close to the scalp and squeeze several times by clenching and releasing your fists. Then, still grasping your hair by the roots, move your fists backward and forward so that your scalp slides across your skull. Repeat these actions all over your head.

166. **TRY A PEBBLE FOOT MASSAGE** to relax and revive you after a long day. Cover the bottom of a shallow tub or bowl with a layer of round pebbles (or marbles). Pour half a cup of hot, salty water over it (as hot as you can handle) and add a few drops of your favourite essential oil (peppermint, with its antiseptic and cooling properties, is ideal for this). Put your feet in the tub and roll them over the pebbles, administering gentle pressure to your soles.

167. **STROKE A CAT** or another furry animal. Studies have shown that stroking pets is therapeutic, as unconditional love is exchanged through contact. It can also reduce high blood pressure.

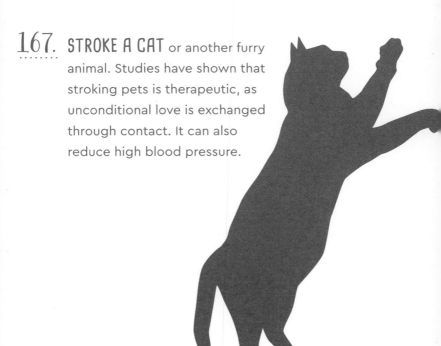

ENERGY TECHNIQUES

168. **CONNECTION SHIATSU** remedies short, shallow breathing caused by stress. Lie on your back and place the palm of one hand on your abdomen, the palm of the other on your chest. Hold for one minute. This will stimulate the flow of chi (vital energy) between your lungs and your kidneys (the "seat" of anxiety), helping you to relax and breathe more deeply.

169. **DEVELOP BREATH AWARENESS.** There is a close relationship between the pattern of our breathing and our state of mind – breathing tends to be shallow and rapid when we are anxious, deep and slow when we are relaxed. By becoming more aware of our breathing, we can consciously alter the pattern to bring us to a more relaxed state of body and mind. Begin by lying on your back, eyes closed, breathing through your nose. Place one hand on your chest and one on your abdomen, and focus on your hands as they rise and fall, reflecting the rhythm and depth of your breathing.

170. **THE HUMMING-BEE BREATH** creates a sound like that of a bee. Humming causes a vibration in the body that is soothing and nurturing, bringing an overall sense of wellbeing. To practise this technique, sit in a comfortable position and take a long, steady in-breath. On the out-breath, hum gently, keeping your jaw relaxed. Continue to hum on every out-breath, allowing the sound to vibrate in the different areas of your face and head. Continue for eight to twelve breaths.

171. **ROAR LIKE A LION.** Based on a yoga technique, this is an excellent way to release tension and stress. First take a deep breath, expanding your ribcage as you fill your lungs with air. Then open your mouth and throat as wide as possible and expel the air by contracting your stomach and diaphragm muscles. As you do so make an "Ahh" sound – the louder and longer the better. Repeat three times, allowing yourself to roar with greater force each time.

172. **DO A CAT STRETCH** – a yoga posture that releases tension from the spine, clearing the head and calming the nerves. Begin on all fours with a neutral spine (neither arched down nor hunched), shoulders over hands, hips over knees. As you breathe in, arch your back down and lift your chest and head slightly. As you breathe out, reverse the movement, curving your spine up and tilting your pelvis beneath you. Repeat this sequence six times.

173. **BREATHE THROUGH YOUR FEET** to help you feel more grounded in times of stress. This exercise can be done whenever your feet are on the ground. As you inhale, imagine you are drawing in air through the soles of your feet, up through your legs and into your torso. As you exhale, imagine the reverse.

174. **LIFT YOUR LEGS.** During inverted yoga postures, the blood rushes down toward the head, bathing the brain in life-giving oxygen. This can energize body and spirit. Lie on your back and lean your legs against a wall. Lightly clasp your hands a few inches above your head, on the floor. Your arms should form a diamond. Breathe deeply and evenly. Lie like this for ten minutes. Performed before bedtime, this position is a good way to encourage restful sleep.

175. **ADOPT THE POSE OF THE CHILD** – a classic yoga resting posture. Based on the foetal position, this pose is calming and nurturing, and particularly helpful if you are experiencing difficult emotions, such as fear or anxiety. Begin by kneeling down, buttocks resting on your heels, with your spine straight and your arms by your sides. Exhaling, fold forward from your hips, bringing your chest to rest on your thighs and your forehead onto the floor. Let your hands slide back toward your feet and your arms rest on the floor. Close your eyes and breathe gently and evenly until any difficult feelings begin to subside.

FEEL RIGHT, LOOK RIGHT

176. GROUND YOURSELF using the basic yoga standing posture. Stand with feet parallel, a few inches apart, aware of contact between the soles of your feet and the earth. Distribute your weight evenly between the balls of your feet and your heels, and between right and left foot. Lengthen your legs by lifting your knees and thighs. Gently draw up your lower abdominal muscles and relax your shoulders and buttocks. Allow your arms to hang, relaxed, at your sides. Breathe deeply, smoothly and evenly.

177. VISUALIZE A GOLDEN THREAD between the top of your head and the heavens. Think of it tightening and lifting you up, making your spine straight, your shoulders lower and your ribcage expand freely. Conjure this image whenever you feel yourself slouching.

178. **PHOTO RAIDERS.** From time to time as you go about the day's business, imagine that two or three paparazzi have materialized from nowhere and are taking pictures of you. Consider what their photographs would say about you. Are there aspects of your posture you wouldn't wish your fans to see? Make any necessary adjustments to the way you are sitting or standing, and see if you can give them better pictures next time they pounce.

179. **MOVE SLOWLY.** We often reveal our anxiety in fast, jerky movements. Slowing down can help calm our nerves. Remember, life is not a race. Some of the most profound experiences unfold slowly.

180. **COMBAT BODY CONSCIOUSNESS** by seeing yourself as 1 per cent body, 99 per cent spirit. Value yourself from inside out, not outside in. Anyone whose opinion matters will accept your appearance and value you for your true inner qualities. Take pride in your appearance, by all means – just as you take pride in your home. But reject anxieties about any aspects of your body you cannot change.

181. **PAMPER YOURSELF.** The body is the vehicle for your spirit, so it's important to take care of it, nurturing it with regular cleansing, scrubbing and moisturizing. If you do this, you will look and feel healthier, which will boost your self-esteem. For this reason, treat yourself to regular haircuts and the occasional pedicure if you fancy it.

EASY EXERCISE

182. **POWER WALKING** – that is, walking at roughly twice the normal speed – is a healthy form of aerobic exercise that can be done en route to work or home, or in your lunch break (you'll need a change of clothes). Or you could do it in a park or in the countryside for a more liberating experience. Between 20 and 30 minutes is the optimum time.

183. **GO FOR A JOG,** preferably around a park or in the countryside to avoid inhaling toxic traffic fumes. As you run, allow yourself to be soothed by the pounding rhythm of your feet. Take time to appreciate your surroundings rather than absorbing yourself entirely in your own thoughts.

184. **SKIP WITH A ROPE** on your patio, backyard or lawn. Although this is an energetic activity, the repetitiveness of the movement and the swinging of the rope have a lulling effect on the body. Reminiscent of the rhyming chants of childhood, jumping rope can transport you back to the innocent play of schooldays.

185. **GO SWIMMING.** Of all sports, swimming probably places least strain on the body – whatever speed you swim, the water will support you, preventing muscle strain or joint injury and allowing you to relax into the movement. Enjoy the sense of weightlessness as you float and the sense of power as you cleave the water. If you feel at home in water you may enjoy scuba-diving, which allows you to explore the magical worlds that co-exist with our own, beneath the water's surface.

186. **GO SKIING** – an exhilarating sport that combines breathtaking scenery with the excitement and release of speed. The challenge is to overcome your fear and lean down the mountain, trusting yourself enough to surrender to the pull of gravity. If the pace of downhill skiing does not appeal, you might prefer cross-country skiing, which tests strength and stamina while bringing the rewards of stunning scenery, increased fitness and a sense of inner satisfaction.

187. **GO FOR A CYCLE RIDE.** If you have access to suitable terrain, cycling can be a wonderfully relaxing activity that allows you to travel further than if you were walking or running, without placing undue strain on the body. It is therefore an ideal way of exploring new places. The flat, sinuous curves of a riverbank are ideal cycling territory and often provide lovely scenery to delight you along the way. If you like to relax your mind by challenging your body, try mountain biking with its tough ascents, rewarded by spectacular views and exhilarating downhill stretches.

188. **LEARN HATHA YOGA** – a form of exercise which aims to unite body, mind and spirit through breath-work and physical postures. A spiritual practice rather than a sport, yoga is not competitive, so work at your own pace and level of suppleness. If you prefer something less physically demanding, try the Chinese art of Tai Chi, in which you work with the energies of the body through slow sequences of continuous movement.

FOOD AND DRINK

189. **DRINK LOTS OF WATER.** Have at least six glasses of filtered, bottled or distilled water daily. This will help flush out impurities and prevent energy-sapping dehydration. A lack of water can seriously affect the function of all our bodily systems, leading to problems such as dry skin, headaches and poor concentration, to name but a few.

190. **EAT FRUIT AND VEGETABLES EVERY DAY.** They bring you into contact with the energies of sun and earth, as well as providing vital nutrients and boosting the immune system.

191. **ADAPT YOUR DIET TO THE SEASON.** In winter, eat heart-warming cooked foods, and in summer opt for lighter meals containing plenty of raw fruit and vegetables.

192. **CUT DOWN ON PROCESSED FOODS** – these are generally a source of "empty" calories, being high in fat and sugar and low in fibre and nutrients. Furthermore, most processed foods contain additives and preservatives, some of which have been clinically proven to cause behavioural disturbances in children and adults. In particular, avoid monosodium glutamate – a food additive that causes insomnia and headaches in certain people.

193. **AVOID STOCKING UP ON FOOD WHEN HUNGRY.** If you do, you may end up buying more than you need, which in turn will encourage you to overeat or throw food away.

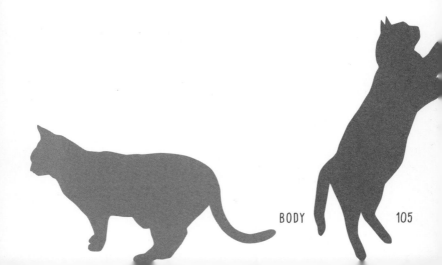

194. **EAT SLOWLY,** relishing every mouthful. Give full attention to the textures and tastes of the food. Appreciate the ambience of the setting – whether familiar or otherwise. This is the body's time: treat your hunger and its satisfaction with respect. About 10 per cent of our daily energy is spent on the digestion, absorption and metabolism of food. After meals, give yourself some quiet time to allow these processes to take place unimpeded.

195. **COOK A MEAL WITH LOVE** – remembering that cooking is creative, and deeply symbolic of the tides of your heart. Our thoughts go into whatever we cook, so it's good to have loving and peaceful thoughts while preparing a meal. Without them all we are doing is refuelling.

196. **INVENT A RECIPE** using at least one ingredient that you have never previously cooked with. Relish the new textures, smells and tastes. If your meal is a success, you can cook it in the future; if not, you can laugh about it with your housemates.

197. **MAKE YOUR FAVOURITE CHILDHOOD** meal for yourself, particularly if you are feeling vulnerable and in need of some comfort and reassurance. It may release all kinds of fascinating memories of distant childhood days.

198. **ENJOY CHOCOLATE.** The main constituent of chocolate is cocoa – a substance first consumed by the Aztecs, who recognized its stimulating and restorative properties, reserving it for warriors, priests and nobles. Today cocoa is known to be rich in antioxidants, which protect us from cancer-promoting free radicals. Good-quality chocolate tends to be high in cocoa and low in sugar, so you can nibble it without feeling guilty.

199. **MAKE YOUR OWN BREAD.** Take out any stress on the dough with vigorous kneading; later, reap the fruits of your efforts with a slice of deliciously scented, freshly-baked bread.

200. **PEEL AN APPLE IN A SINGLE STRIP.** Perform the task slowly, trying to keep the strip thin and of even width. Giving your full concentration to this task will sharpen your senses and clear your mind, enhancing your enjoyment of the apple when you eat it.

201. PERFORM A TEA CEREMONY

to transform your afternoon teatime into a meditative ritual. Make the tea slowly and deliberately, using the best tea set you have. Lay everything out with precision, and with a due sense of everyday sacredness. Take long pauses between each movement, particularly the drinking. Be totally mindful of every movement. You may be surprised to find that such a ceremony has a deeply calming effect. Once you have mastered your personal tea ceremony, invite some friends to join you. Drink tea together in silence. To enhance the calm induced by this ritual, experiment with alternative teas: green tea is soothing and caffeine-free; liquorice tea helps to support adrenal function, thereby reducing stress; and peppermint and ginger teas calm the digestive tract and stomach.

BODY WISDOM

202. TAKE RESPONSIBILITY FOR YOUR OWN HEALTH.

There is a Western tendency to see disease as something to which we fall victim – the disease attacks us and there is nothing we can do to defend ourselves. In fact there is plenty we can do. Taking care of our bodies is perhaps the most important thing. This may seem obvious but all too often we deprive the body of sleep, fuel it with junk food, pollute it with cigarettes and alcohol, fail to exercise it, and then are surprised when the body starts to break down, having lost its ability to fend off disease. To improve our health it is important to look honestly at the ways we mistreat our bodies, and then work to alter those habits. One way to look after the body is to undergo a regular health assessment with a health practitioner – orthodox or complementary – to catch problems early before they develop. If this seems excessive, consider that you would probably give your car an annual service, so why not your body? For the same reason, go for regular eye tests and dental check-ups. The eye test is particularly important if you spend much of your time working at a computer – an activity that can strain the eyes. The dental check-up will ward off decay and gum disease, and keep staining to a minimum.

203. VISIT AN AROMATHERAPIST. Practitioners of aromatherapy use the concentrated essential oils of plants to relieve a range of emotional and physical conditions, including those that are stress-related. These oils can be used alone or in blends for massage, inhalation, compresses, baths and in special burners. If you want to experiment with essential oils on your own, try the following, which are particularly beneficial for relaxation: fruity and apple-like in scent, camomile soothes the nerves and is suitable for sensitive skin; sweet-smelling jasmine acts as an antidepressant, and is particularly helpful for the treatment of post-natal depression; lavender, which has a fresh fragrance, has antiseptic, analgesic and calming properties, and can be used to treat headaches, insomnia and depression; petitgrain has a sweet aroma and acts as a sedative and treatment for anxiety and insomnia; exotic ylang ylang has antidepressant, sedative and antiseptic properties and helps to allay anxiety. You can dilute these (or other essential oils) in a carrier oil for massage, place a few drops in the bath or on a pillow, or buy an oil burner to scent your bedroom.

204. **RECOVER PROPERLY** from illness, even if you have to take time off work or cancel plans. Don't feel guilty if you let people down: you need to take care of yourself in order to take care of others.

205. **KNOW YOUR BODY CLOCK.** We all have different natural phases of high and low energy. If you recognize these and do high-energy and low-energy tasks at the appropriate times, you will make the most of your day, both creatively and practically.

206. **OVERCOME WINTER BLUES.** During dark winter months it's common to suffer from fatigue, irritability and attention lapses. These are the symptoms of SAD (seasonal affective disorder) – a hormonal imbalance that occurs as a result of inadequate exposure to natural light. The cure is to spend no less than one hour a day outside, and to install full-spectrum lamps indoors.

207. BALANCE FEMALE HORMONES NATURALLY

by eating estrogenic foods such as soya, tofu, sweet potatoes, broccoli, cauliflower and Brussels sprouts. This will help tackle the symptoms of PMS (pre-menstrual syndrome), such as mood swings, headaches, breast pain and water retention, that afflict many women each month. Other helpful measures that you can take just before your period include cutting down on foods with high salt content, such as pretzels, salted peanuts and processed meats; and taking a high-strength vitamin B complex to help your liver process oestrogens, vitamin E, calcium and magnesium to help to reduce the symptoms of tension and keep you calm, and GLA (gamma linoleic acid), which is found abundantly in evening primrose oil, to reduce breast pain.

The
Peaceful
Home

LIGHT, SHADE AND COLOUR

208. **USE MIRRORS** to maximize the flow of energizing natural light through your home. Light promotes physical vitality and mental alertness. Its absence can cause vitamin D deficiencies, as well as fatigue, depression or irritability. What better antidote than a few mirrors carefully positioned to illuminate dark corners? Many people prefer to avoid seeing reflections of themselves as they move around the house or apartment. This problem is usually easy to solve by angling mirrors downward; or positioning them at higher or lower levels than your eyes; or just by judging the sightlines carefully. Another approach is to place a potted plant in front of a mirror. This spreads the light while at the same time fragmenting unwanted reflections. It also has the advantage of doubling the impact of the plant. Use hinged mirrors to increase the multiplication even further.

209. **FOLLOW THE SUN** on its journey around the room on a sunny day. Notice how the light quality changes depending on the angle at which sunlight falls through the window. Plan your interior décor to make the most of such daily and seasonal changes. The peaceful home is one that you have created around the given cycles of natural lighting.

210. **USE SHEER FABRICS** as curtains or shades to diffuse and soften the light where appropriate (for example, in living rooms and possibly dining rooms), creating an ethereal mood that combines seclusion and mystery. In other rooms (such as bedrooms) you might choose instead to use thick drapes or shutters to allow you to block out daylight completely, helping you to generate an intimate, relaxing mood.

211. OPT FOR FLEXIBLE ARTIFICIAL LIGHTING – not just a single light source but a number of alternative light sources at different heights in every room. The ideal is to have a choice of lighting permutations, including individual pools of light around chairs and occasional tables, some directional lighting (for example, to provide good light to work by), and some light purely for ambient mood.

212. CANDLES offer a wonderful source of mood lighting – as well as a suitable focus for a simple meditation. Look out for interesting holders, such as pierced-tin cylinders, which can cast a soothing light show onto nearby walls. You can also float candles in decorative bowls filled with water to establish an ambience of gentle mysticism. (Never leave a candle unattended; and be sure that the flame is at a safe distance from any object or material, whether flammable or not.)

213. **USE COLOURS STRATEGICALLY,** bearing in mind their impact on mood. Cooler hues tend to be calming, warmer hues tend to be stimulating. Bear in mind the psychological and spiritual meanings associated with colours:

RED is associated with fire, so that a patch of red in a room can be a subtle substitute for a blazing hearth.

ORANGE is linked with spirituality and transcendence, and is a good colour for meditators.

YELLOW, associated with sunlight, promotes optimism.

GREEN connects us with nature and instils a sense of harmony.

BLUE, the colour of an untroubled sky, suggests openness, freedom and tranquillity.

INDIGO, reminiscent of ocean depths, adds mystery to an interior.

VIOLET, symbolic of the "inner eye", the centre of spiritual vision, can guide us on the inward quest.

214. **MIX HUES JUDICIOUSLY** to create a harmonious effect – either different colours in matching tones or a narrower range of colours in different tones. Neutral hues, such as off-whites, creams, buffs or greys, provide a subdued background to off-set splashes of more vibrant hue – a safe option for those who are uncertain of their colour sense.

215. **USE PATTERNS WITH RESTRAINT** – too many patterns of different kinds may clash with each other and subtly disturb your mental equilibrium. On the other hand, rich patterns can conjure up calm through their associations with nature or with a pre-industrial lifestyle. Many patterns are Eastern in origin (think of Eastern carpets), and so conjure up a relaxed ambience for Westerners inspired by Eastern wisdom.

MANAGING YOUR SPACES

216. **CLEAR OUT YOUR CLUTTER.** Sorting out your wardrobes, drawers and cupboards and throwing out all that accumulated rubbish will allow the things you need and treasure to breathe. Above all, you'll know that there's order even in hidden places – a good analogy for the virtue that shines within the spirit.

217. **GIVE TO A THRIFT STORE** or charity collection – a great way to combine a clear-out with a generous civic gesture. Wash any clothes before you give them away; mend any tears; replace any missing buttons – all these selfless acts will increase the karmic value of your donation.

218. **DO LAUNDRY MINDFULLY** and turn a household chore into a kind of meditation exercise. When the clothes come from the dryer, enjoy the feel and the fresh smell of the warm fabric as you fold each item. If done with attention to detail, by the time your task is finished you should be feeling thoroughly peaceful and relaxed.

219. **REPAIR THINGS** when possible, especially clothes: today we live in a throwaway culture, but our unwillingness to tolerate even minor imperfections is an unfortunate attachment. Take a more relaxed attitude and make do with things that are less than pristine but still in perfect working order.

220. **HAVE A TINY JOB DAY.** Do all the niggling little chores around the house that are pricking your conscience on a daily basis. Knocking off half a dozen or so little jobs on the same day is a certain way to nurture good feelings about yourself.

221. **TOUCH UP THE PAINTWORK.** A few hours spent spot-treating scuffs and marks will enhance your home environment and subtly boost your peace of mind.

222. **IRON OUT YOUR CREASES.** Even the most mundane of tasks, such as ironing, can be an exercise in calm. Imagine as you iron that the creases in your clothes are worries about life's insolubles. As you smoothe out each crease, visualize one of these worries losing its sharp edges.

223. CLEAN YOUR WINDOWS. Smears or other marks on glass may be a trivial blemish, but they interpose themselves between yourself and the outside world and are thus a constant reminder of minor neglect and therefore subliminally stressful. Use a squeegee or paper towels with a proprietary window cleaner. Wash the inside surface with up-and-down swipes and the outside with cross swipes: that way if a streak remains, you'll know which side of the glass it's on.

224. **TREAT YOUR CAR WELL** – it's small enough for you to be able to maintain it as a totally clean and clutter-free environment. Given the hours you spend driving, this is a much more relaxing approach than treating your car as a dump to carry the overspill of household clutter. Respect the car's inner needs, too: have it serviced regularly; fix minor mishaps (like a broken wing mirror) as soon as you can, though without getting stressed about it.

225. **REARRANGE THE FURNITURE.** Experiment with new circulation routes. Break the grip of habit upon your domestic surroundings. Unless you set aside time to put deliberate thought into the optimum arrangement for your needs, you may miss good opportunities for making the home more user-friendly.

POSITIVE ENERGIES

226. **CIRCULATION ROUTES,** such as halls, landings and stairs, are like the meridians, or energy lines, that thread through the body carrying chi (vital energy): both must be kept clear of blockages if the energy is to flow naturally. So avoid clutter in these parts of the home and place a ban on oversized furniture.

227. **KEEP THE MIDDLE OF A ROOM CLEAR** to create a sense of spaciousness and energy. This is an important principle of Vastu Vidya (the ancient Indian spiritual tradition of architecture and placement), which asserts that furniture placed in the sacred centre of a room impedes the flow of energy (prana) through the space.

228. **THE SHAPE OF YOUR DINING TABLE,** according to Vedic principles, affects the ambience of the room. Square or rectangular represents the Earth element, and thus has a grounding effect. Circular represents the Water element, prompting lively conviviality. You may not be able to switch easily, but it's good to know what influences are afoot!

229. **ORIENT YOUR BED** so that your head points south when you sleep. According to the Indian tradition of Vastu Vidya (see point 227, opposite), the body possesses an electromagnetic field like a magnet, with the head as the north pole. Aligning this with the electromagnetic field of the Earth is believed to promote restful sleep. As opposite poles attract, this involves positioning your bed so that your head points toward the south pole.

230. **RESCUE HARMLESS INSECTS** trapped in your house, instead of thoughtlessly despatching them – they weren't trying to walk off with your silver! Respect nature, even when it trespasses.

231. **CRYSTALS** placed around your home will absorb negativity and promote a happy, harmonious atmosphere. Choose crystals that are rough-cut rather than polished. Before arranging them in the home, place them outside in a bowl of water for 24 hours: this practice cleanses and re-energizes the crystals, and should be repeated every month or so. The fascination of crystals comes from their earth-born beauty; but, in addition, they are a powerful metaphor for the spirit's transcendence of the flesh, or, at a more mundane level, the potential for transformation in all of us. Here are some brief profiles of some of the most popular types:
CLEAR QUARTZ, also known as "white quartz" or "rock crystal", can lift us into a lighter, more joyful state.
AVENTURINE, a beautiful green stone, clears turbulent thoughts and purifies the emotions.
ROSE QUARTZ, associated with love, gently releases emotional blockages.
YELLOW CALCITE can help to lift our spirits out of depression, bringing inner strength and peace.

THE FEEL-GOOD HOME

232. NAME YOUR HOUSE OR APARTMENT. Choose a name that conjures up a positive image – for example, connoting calm, or strength, or inspiration. The subtle aura of the name will embrace you as you re-enter the home.

233. WEAR SLIPPERS AT HOME – keep them by the front door so that you can slip into them when you enter. You might even consider having different pairs of slippers for different rooms of the house – the ultimate in Zen-like respect for floor surfaces.

234. **A SYMBOL OF TRANQUILLITY** in your entrance hall or just outside your front door will remind you to unwind when you come home. Consider hanging a plaque inscribed with a Chinese character, or an image of a dove. Pay respect to the emblem as you pass by. A symbol of longevity also makes a good focal point for an entranceway, and there are many to choose from, especially in traditional Chinese belief. Examples are: the crane, a bird thought by the Chinese to live for a thousand years or more; the phoenix, the legendary bird that supposedly renewed itself in fire; the carp (which in its ornamental form can, of course, be embodied as real fish in a suitable pool); and the hare, elephant, deer, stork, toad, tortoise, turtle and peach. The colour green and the stone jade have similar connotations. Symbols of abundance, such as the pomegranate and the cornucopia (horn of plenty), would also be suitable in this position.

235. **INTRODUCE CURVES** into a room, for a softening effect. Curved shapes are gentler on the eye than angular ones, and invite repose. They can be three-dimensional (as in a round side-table with scrolled feet) or two-dimensional (as in a pattern on fabric or wallpaper).

236. **REFLECT THE SEASONS.** Bring into your home the tones and textures of nature to reflect the changing seasons, using candles and scents, plants and flowers that embody these times of year. Spring is fresh and soft; summer, heady and bright; autumn, darker and more abundant; winter, rich and heavy.

237. **TURN DOWN THE RADIO** from time to time so that you can hear the voices but not what they are saying – the volume should be quiet enough to createa low, soothing murmur.

238. **MAKE A QUILT OF LOVE** – a patchwork quilt using patches of fabric that hold special meaning for you, such as a square of your father's checked shirt, a cushion cover from your first marital home, and so on. This project combines the relaxing activity of sewing, the magpie pleasures of improvised assembly, and the celebratory instinct. Once the quilt is completed, you'll be able to wrap yourself in happy memories every night.

239. **PLANT SOME SEEDS** or bulbs, or perhaps a seedling or young plant – an antidote to the temptation to see your garden as merely a place that requires endless maintenance in the form of weeding, pruning and chopping back. Being able to see something of your own making (or at least facilitating) grow to maturity is one of the privileges of being human. And in nourishing these growing things we learn to still the distractions of the ego.

240. **MAKE A ZEN GARDEN** in a little sandpit with artfully placed rocks. Rake the sand around the rocks. Meditate on the beautiful pattern you have created. (Use gravel, if you wish, as a low-maintenance alternative to sand.) Or make an indoor version inside a shallow container, perhaps on the kitchen windowsill. Use an old kitchen fork to rake the sand.

241. **GROW YOUR OWN VEGETABLES.** This brings a double pleasure: a degree of self-sufficiency, combined with the joy of giving away any surplus to family, friends or neighbours.

242. **PLANT A TREE.** It's good for our mental health to take actions that require patience before results are seen – even stretching beyond our own lifetimes. If you don't have a garden, ask a friend who does if you may plant one in theirs; or approach the local parks department and make a donation to posterity.

243. **FEED THE BIRDS** in your garden during winter, using nuts in a hanging feeder designed to discourage cats or birds of prey. Helping wildlife in times of need is always good karma. If a cat does catch a bird, don't be too harsh on it – the creature is hardwired this way! Also, set up a bird bath and enjoy watching the birds splash about vigorously in the water.

244. **MAKE AN ARBOUR IN YOUR GARDEN** or backyard by trailing fast-growing climbers over a simple timber framework. If the climbers are scented (for example, honeysuckle), so much the better. Place a garden seat beneath your arbour to give you some relaxing shade in the summer months.

245. **TALK TO YOUR NEIGHBOURS** and help to encourage a community of mutual support. A network of friendly neighbours offers the potential for dealing effectively with a whole range of difficulties – from letting an electrician into your property while you're at work to watering your plants while you're away on vacation.

246. **GIVE A SPARE KEY** to a neighbour. This act of faith will be appreciated and has the added benefit that you need never be accidentally locked out of your home again.

247. **WELCOME NEWCOMERS** to the area. Ask them what you can do to help. Surprise them with a moving-in present.

248. **TAKE A DETOUR** on the way home, just to vary your routine. That way, you get to know your area, with better understanding of what it has to offer in terms of practical and leisure facilities.

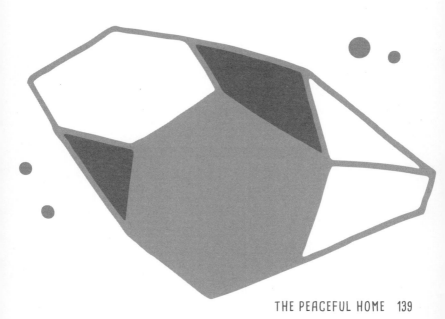

249. VIEW SPRING BLOSSOM

– a pastime of the Japanese who celebrate the onset of spring by picnicking under the flowering cherry trees. Sip herbal tea with a friend. Write a poignant haiku about the blossom. Appreciate other spring or summer highlights as well. In some areas you might go on a magnolia safari during a week-long period in spring. Magnolia trees are beautiful, with open, candle-like flowers. In the autumn, relish fall colours. Write a poem about autumn, as John Keats did.

250. BE A LOCAL HISTORIAN. Find relaxing fascination in the history of your town or street.

Work

PERSONAL SPACE

251. **CLEAR YOUR DESK EVERY EVENING** – file your papers away in their proper place, tidy pens and other stationery, transfer handwritten notes to a more permanent place for storage. This may be the last thing you feel like doing at close of play, but it will help you to begin work the following day with a clear head. An extension of this is the pre-lunch clear-out. Not only does this set you up for the afternoon, but it has the added advantage of making it more obvious when someone has put something on your desk during your lunch break.

252. **TEND A PLANT** in the workplace – buy one specially if necessary. Check the plant every day to see whether it requires watering or the removal of dead leaves. Nurture has a place in every working environment. Having started with plants, you may begin to see your nurturing influence spread to other people too.

253. **KEEP A BOWL OF FRUIT ON YOUR DESK** to provide yourself with three things: a source of healthy snacks, a still-life to enjoy in brief contemplative breaks, and a collection of small generous offerings for colleagues or visitors who come for a discussion or a brief meeting with you.

254. **KEEP SOMETHING ABSURD OR INCONGRUOUS ON YOUR DESK** to tickle your sense of humour and remind you that there is more to life than the stresses of work.

DOING A GOOD JOB

255. **DON'T KNOCK ROUTINE.** True, it can get you down sometimes, but why not throw yourself into the activity rather than worrying about how drearily familiar it seems? Routine makes us feel safe and provides a strong foundation on which to build our dreams.

256. **KEEP A DAY-PER-PAGE DIARY** for noting down miscellaneous details you need to remember; when you wish to retrieve the information at a later date, all you have to do is recall roughly when you made the note and thumb through the diary until you find the entry. If a temporary record is sufficient, it's usually quicker to deal with memoranda in this way than to type up notes and file them among your other memos and letters.

257. CHOOSE ONE OF THE FOUR DS: Do it, Delegate it, Dump it or Defer it. The ability to balance your work load, delegating, dumping or deferring what cannot be done immediately, is an important management skill for ensuring maximum efficiency. When choosing between options, remember that when delegating you retain ultimate responsibility for the task, and are therefore also responsible for supporting your subordinate in completing it to your satisfaction. By contrast, when dumping, you are assessing that no one need take any action – a decision for which you are willing to take full responsibility. Deferral is the option for non-urgent tasks that you will have to do yourself. Although, in our personal lives, we sometimes view deferral as a sign of self-delusion, at work it is part of prioritizing – a valid strategy for dealing with a crowded in-tray.

258. MAKE A "LIMBO BOX" for papers you are not sure whether to keep or not, cleaning the box out periodically. This gives you time to decide whether a paper is required, freeing you from the need to hang on to everything, or the angst of having thrown out something you should have kept. At the same time as sorting your limbo box, take the opportunity to make sure that your filing is up to date.

259. DO ONE TASK EACH DAY THAT YOU DO NOT LIKE DOING. There are unpleasant or boring aspects to every job. By doing a task that you dislike each day, rather than putting them all off, you spread the load, avoiding a backlog of unpleasant tasks preying on your conscience.

260. COMPLETE SMALL TASKS ADEQUATELY rather than perfectly when you feel overwhelmed by your workload. This will allow you to concentrate on the most important tasks at hand, ensuring that they are completed to a high standard.

261. GIVE YOURSELF MINI-DEADLINES each day for the completion of potentially open-ended tasks, such as dealing with correspondence or managing emails.

262. **MAKE NOTES ON YOUR MISTAKES** and discoveries when performing a difficult task for the first time. Refer to these notes when you repeat the task to avoid making the same mistakes twice and to aid you in decision-making.

YOU AND YOUR COLLEAGUES

263. ALLOW YOUR WHOLE SELF INTO THE WORKPLACE.
Obviously, work is not the place for letting all your
emotions hang out, but that doesn't mean you're
expected to hide your true self. Be honest about
how you're feeling. Allow colleagues to see the
whole self concentrating its attention, during the
working day, on the job in hand to the best of
your ability.

264. RECOGNIZE TRANSFERENCE – the psychologist's
term for the process by which we project emotions
connected with a particular issue onto the nearest
available target, usually an innocent party. A common
example of this in the workplace is when someone
takes out their frustration with their boss on a junior.
Becoming aware that you are transferring your
emotions onto another is the first step to avoiding
this pattern.

265. **TAKE CRITICISM** into your mind, as though inviting a stranger into your home. Talk to it. See if you can find something in common with it, a perspective that you share. Use that common ground to build on and improve what you are doing. Treating criticism as a personal affront and therefore rejecting it out of hand creates anger and tension, and also prevents you from absorbing useful feedback.

266. **LET OTHERS LEARN FROM YOUR MISTAKES,** as well as yourself. Creating a workplace in which workers are encouraged to report their mistakes without fear of reprimand not only improves the atmosphere but also means that workers are able to pool their experiences so that everyone can learn from each others' misjudgements. This results in a more efficient workplace.

267. SHOW AN INTEREST IN OTHERS' LIVES. This will prevent you from falling into the trap of seeing people merely as their roles. Remember, everyone is capable of surprising you!

268. BE GRACIOUS. Sometimes the people we work with become so familiar to us that we take them for granted, leaving out the civilities that make for quality relationships. Remember your manners. People flower when treated with grace and respect.

269. VOLUNTEER FOR A SOCIAL ROLE WITHIN YOUR COMPANY. For example, you might go on a first-aid course, or organize cinema trips for as many colleagues as wish to attend. Such activities enable you to relate to your colleagues in a social as well as professional context, humanizing the workplace and breaking down artificial divisions between you and your fellow workers.

270. **TAKE AN EYE-BREAK** every ten minutes when working at a computer screen. Just allow your eyes to roam around the room and adjust to the longer distance.

271. **INTERLOCK YOUR FINGERS AND STRETCH YOUR ARMS ABOVE YOUR HEAD** for a quick-fix office stretch. As you do so, lean back in your chair (keeping all the feet on the floor), stretch yourself upward and breathe slowly and deeply for about 20 seconds.

272. **DO A SEATED TWIST** at your desk. Sit sideways on your chair and, on an out-breath, turn your upper torso toward the chair's back, holding the back with both hands. Maintain this position for three to six breaths, then repeat on the other side. This gentle stretch helps to ease any lower back pain that results from sitting still for too long. It also helps to unblock the mind.

273. **VISIT AN ART GALLERY** during your lunch hour. Find a picture that is both relaxing and satisfying to look at, and contemplate it for at least five full minutes. It could be an expansive landscape, an abstract work painted in tranquil hues, or a religious painting expressing transcendence. Return to work with a postcard of the work to cue the memory of this peaceful encounter.

274. **GET TO KNOW A PARK** near your workplace. Spend warm and pleasant hours there in your lunch breaks. Pay attention to the seasonal changes in the vista. Adopt a favourite bench. Talk to the gardeners. Enjoy the relaxing two-fold experience of being amid nature at the heart of the community.

275. **HANG YOUR WORK ROLE** on the coat-stand each evening as you leave. This simple visualization will encourage you to leave the frustrations of work behind you in the office rather than taking them home. Do this even if you plan to work at home that evening – it will create a healthy break between the working day and the working evening.

276. **WEEK OFF/WEEK ON/WEEK OFF** can be a good approach to a two-week vacation. That way you get four holiday weekends rather than three. And the middle week back at work helps to prevent a backlog of jobs building up.

People

GIVING AND SHARING

277. **INVENT A CROSSWORD** for a friend where all the answers are good qualities that you see in them. As they solve the puzzle, they'll travel on a voyage of self-discovery and self-esteem.

278. **GIVE PRESENTS FOR NO REASON** except to show the value you place upon a relationship. Such presents, falling out of a clear blue sky, often give the most satisfaction – to giver and recipient.

279. **PLAN A "ROYAL" SURPRISE** for your partner or a friend, or a close relative. Take care of all the practicalities. Just tell them where to come and when – and what to wear, if relevant. The treat can be anything from dinner on a boat to a visit to an owl sanctuary. Make your companion feel like a king or queen.

280. TEACH SOMEONE

your special skill – whether it's art or algebra, birdwatching or ballroom dancing, yoga or yachting. There are few greater gifts you can offer. Combine this with the gifts of patience and understanding – and tolerance of a beginner's inevitable mistakes.

281. SURPRISE SOMEONE you don't know very well with

an act of kindness. A good example would be to pay for an elderly person's shopping next time you're in the supermarket. Or bring your bad-tempered neighbour a souvenir T-shirt back from your vacation.

282. **GIVE BLOOD.** Few actions offer such an enormous return for such little sacrifice. As you give blood, appreciate your own health and send the recipient your good wishes for his or her speedy recovery. Similarly, carry a donor card. It's good to know you'll continue to improve others' lives after your physical existence is over.

283. **DROP ALL YOUR LOOSE CHANGE** into a charity collecting box. As you do so, briefly visualize the money doing its practical work of helping – whether buying bread for the starving or contributing to the purchase of hospital equipment. Relieved of the coins, you should feel lighter – a burden has been lifted.

LOVE AND COMPASSION

284. **SEND OUT LOVE TO FAMILY OR FRIENDS.** Visualize a loved one happily cocooned in positive love energy radiating from your spirit. This love energy carries profound wishes of happiness, health, security and peace. Hold this visualization in your mind for a few minutes. Resolve that you will make it come true as much as possible within your relationship. As a variation on this theme, wish happiness, health, security and peace to acquaintances you like, then proceed to acquaintances to whom you are indifferent, then people you actively dislike. This is a modern variation on the Tibetan loving kindness meditation.

285. KEEP YOUR COMPASSION CLEAR. Whenever you see suffering in others, resist the temptation to suffer with them: it never helps. Instead, disconnect from the person's suffering while remaining mentally and empathetically engaged with it. Disconnecting prevents your power from being drained, so that you can concentrate on giving the help that is needed. This is compassion in action.

286. PUT PEOPLE AT EASE in embarrassing situations. Embarrassment is a mild form of distress and one that can often be remedied easily to generate good feelings all around.

287. **FORGIVE FREELY.** Forgiveness is the natural condition of the spirit, a petal on the flower of love. When we forgive we are giving out positive energy: some of that energy, at the deepest level, will always be gratefully received and aptly used.

288. **PRACTISE DRISHTI,** the Hindu vision of benevolence. Send the energy of benevolence through your eyes toward others. Our eyes are transmitters of subtle energy, and that energy touches everyone and everything we look at. Give drishti to your friends, family, neighbours, colleagues – and to the world.

289. BOW TO THE LIGHT WITHIN THE OTHER. A

traditional Indian greeting is to hold both palms together in front of you, as if in prayer, and greet or say farewell to someone by speaking the word "namaste", meaning: "I bow to light within you." It is a gesture of the deepest respect. Use it whenever you feel that the customary salutations are inadequate to express your regard. Other forms of greeting that increase the world's stock of goodwill might include: "Peace to you," or simply "Peace!" This is a tradition of Muslim countries. Hawaiians use the exuberant, life-affirming greeting "Aloha!" A variation is "Aloha Akoa!" meaning "God's love". The Jewish greeting "yasher koach" recognizes good effort and expresses a wish for continued strength. In Thailand people give "wai" by joining their palms together at chin level and bowing as a sign of respect, especially for age and reverence. The lower your graceful Japanese bow, the more respectful you're being. The Mediterranean tradition of kissing each other several times on alternate cheeks instantly affirms your bond.

RESPONSIBILITY AND RESPECT

290. **REJECT BLAME** using this affirmation: "It is not what you say or do to me that makes me feel this way, it is what I do with what you say or do to me that makes me feel this way." An alternative affirmation might emphasize peace: "I will not allow hurt to fester inside me. I hereby declare peace in my heart." Or you could choose to end a cold war by a unilateral declaration: "I break the chain of blame. I require nothing in return."

291. **KEEP YOUR PROMISES.** Each time we break a promise or commitment, even to ourselves, we chip away at our claim to be a responsible, self-aware person. Giving your word is a serious undertaking, even on trivial matters. Don't make a promise if the situation warrants a more open-ended response. Negotiate, if necessary, a looser arrangement.

292. **CULTIVATE GRATITUDE** even for things that you have taken for granted in the past – even the food we eat is a gift. From gratitude comes the realization that we already have enough. When we feel that we have enough, we are willing to let go – and in doing so we are well placed to receive more.

293. **RECOGNIZE THE PRIVILEGE** of meeting or spending time with someone who has a keen intellect, or is well-read, or well-travelled, or otherwise accomplished. Don't think of them as superior, and don't be daunted by them. You are fortunate to encounter them – but remember that everyone has as much to give as to receive.

294. LEARN SPREZZATURA – a virtue prized by Italians in the Renaissance. It means a kind of considerate, modest casualness, an unwillingness to put your own comfort or convenience in the foreground. For example, imagine that you've spent all day cooking a meal for a friend who's due to visit you that evening. When the friend turns up at your door, she says she has already eaten, and would you like to go to a bar? Readily and happily, you agree to this. You say nothing about the meal you have slaved over. You are showing sprezzatura.

295. **AVOID CORRECTING PEOPLE.** Mentally we often spend energy correcting other people's appearance, speech, opinions, enthusiasms – everything. It's as if they were a text and we were an editor. Don't do this. Correction is unreal and pointless, as well as being a potential source of tension.

296. **DON'T GOSSIP.** Gossip often starts with a betrayal of trust. On its travels it distorts grotesquely. People gossip to be admired for their access to private knowledge. And gossip can end up hurting people. Four good reasons not to do it. Besides, you're better than that.

DIFFICULTIES

297. **SEE ALL RELATIONSHIPS AS FRUITFUL** – if only because they bring you self-knowledge. Don't fret over a past relationship that didn't work out as you'd hoped: instead, consider what you learned from it.

298. **BREAK THE CHAIN OF BLAME.** Some people are bound to each other by bonds of mutual blame – and the result is usually stress on both sides. Unilaterally withdraw negative feelings from someone you've blamed until now. Remain positive toward them even if you know they don't reciprocate. It may take them more time, but even if they continue to bear you ill-will, no matter! Be karmic: give without expectation.

299. **BAN CRITICISM OF EACH OTHER,** of any kind, open or implied, by mutual agreement: an ideal plan when a relationship needs a bit of help. In other words, go on a love-diet where only loving feelings are allowed – niggles and sarcastic jibes are taboo. Rule-breakers pay whatever fines have been pre-arranged – whether hugs, chores or contributions to a charity box.

300. **THINK WHILE YOU SPEAK** if you find yourself disagreeing with somebody – or even if you're in accord. Pause if necessary to decide what you really believe. This takes some practice, as many people are unable to think while debating: instead they offer ready-made views. Remember, you needn't talk faster just because someone else is chattering away – just speak at your own usual pace. In difficult conversations, feel free to ask for a time-out while you think things through. Halting the dialogue for a minute or two is a good way to take the tension out of an argument.

301. **DISPEL A SPIKY "AURA"** or combative attitude by imagining that the one thing it can't make an impact on is a combination of saintly patience and confidence in your own silent strength. Summon these qualities from within yourself. The spikiness won't disappear, but the spikes will certainly lose their power to prick you.

302. **A MEDLEY OF LEAVES.** Visualize your hands cupped and holding autumn leaves of various hues. The leaves symbolize the mixed feelings you have for a friend, colleague or member of your family, or a current situation you are facing. Imagine that a gust of wind blows all the leaves out of your hands, scattering them at your feet. With the contradictions gone, you are now free to make a fresh start.

COMMUNICATION

303. **SHAKE HANDS FIRMLY** – not too limp, and not too concentratedly sincere (some people find the double handshake alarming). Look the person right in the eyes as you make hand contact. Let your touch be a two-way channel of good will.

304. **LISTEN TO PEOPLE.** By attending to others we stay in balance with them. Actively listen to what others are saying, in all your relationships, however casual or temporary. Read people's gestures, too, as body language can speak volumes.

305. ASK YOUR PARTNER ABOUT HIS OR HER PAST.

Even after you've known them a long time, there'll still be much to discover. And sharing memories can strengthen your bond.

306. SHARE THE COOKING – time spent working with someone in the kitchen can be intimate, and at the same time a good opportunity to unburden yourself of whatever is weighing heavily on your mind.

307. **TAKE ONE FULL BREATH** before you speak in response to anyone. This allows you to be responsive rather than merely reactive; and to fully listen to and understand what the other has said, rather than deafly pursuing your own agenda.

308. **LOOK UP AN OLD FRIEND.** Every time we move house or change jobs we lose contact with friends. Re-establish links with someone you miss. Enjoy the pleasures of reunion.

309. **DON'T SWALLOW A COMPLIMENT:** speak it, as soon the thought occurs to you. To hold back on praise is tantamount to undervaluing someone.

310. **OPEN OUT SELF-DIALOGUE.** We all continue long conversations with ourselves, in our heads. But wouldn't it be a pity to waste our best insights on an audience of one? Don't bottle up your best thoughts: share them and let others benefit. This might seem a bit strange to begin with – as if you're letting people into your inner sanctum for the first time. But you'll find that a dialogue of comfortable intimacy is soon established, its boundaries tacitly agreed. As always, giving brings gifts in its wake.

311. **LEARN SIGNING** and work with the deaf on a voluntary basis. This is communication par excellence – how good it feels to help others overcome their communication problems!

312. **SAY "GOOD MORNING" TO PEOPLE.** Old-fashioned manners will never lose their value. Smile and be bright while saying it – all too often good-mornings are mumbled by people who don't really feel that way. Say your good-morning sincerely, as a heartfelt wish.

313. **SMILE OUTWARDLY.** Even when you're feeling low, smiling at someone triggers the release of endorphins ("happy hormones") that will help to boost your mood. Try smiling at strangers, anyone with whom you make eye contact – you may be surprised how often the smile is returned. And an outward smile often engenders the appropriate inner feelings: although human beings normally operate from the inside out, sometimes outside in is a worthwhile strategy for enhancing your inner peace.

314. TALK TO STRANGERS – and not only at parties. An Irish proverb says that there's no such thing as strangers, only friends you've yet to meet. With each encounter, try to find one acquaintance, possession or belief you have in common. You'll often be surprised how many fascinating correspondences you can find.

315. BRING AN OPEN MIND to new people or places, or to new experiences: like a parachute, a mind functions better when it is open. Your way is only one of many ways. Open-minded people tend to find more to enjoy and less to be disappointed by.

316. CHOOSE GOOD COMPANY. Undoubtedly, we are influenced by the energy and calm (these are far from mutually exclusive qualities) of the people around us. Peaceful, self-possessed, independent-minded people often allow us to see our own lives in a fresh perspective. And, of course, good-natured people, who like a joke, are always going to exert a relaxing influence.

317. BE GOOD COMPANY and help your friends to be good company too by valuing them and boosting their self-esteem. Show them that you love to let their talents shine.

<u>318.</u> **TAKE PHOTOS** of friends and family, without worrying too much about composition. The important thing is to capture something real and spontaneous about your subjects, and this only works by chance. Don't be upset if some of the photos turn out less than perfect: a snapshot is a kind of lottery, with some happy yesses and many invaluable maybes.

Creativity and Play

THE ARTS

319. GET LOST IN A FUGUE – an intricate and satisfying form of musical composition. Listen to the piece several times in order to trace each individual strand or voice within the composition as they weave together in counterpoint to form a magical tapestry of sound. J S Bach is the acknowledged master of the form – try his *Art of Fugue*, a collection of 48 fugues and preludes for the piano, or the "Sanctus" in Verdi's choral work, *Requiem*.

320. BE A KITCHEN-SINK MUSICIAN. The kitchen offers a wealth of opportunities for spontaneous music-making. Experiment with using wooden spoons and metal whisks for drumsticks, the kitchen sink, if it's made of stainless steel, as a large steel drum, and saucepans for side-drums. Create a xylophone out of bottles filled with varying amounts of water and play them with metal spoons, or scrape a vegetable grater with a fork.

321. **JOIN A CHOIR.** Singing is invigorating and cathartic. Sing with others and the benefits are multiplied. Join a choir and you'll improve your teamwork and listening skills, experience the exhilaration of live performance, and gain access to a great repertoire of choral music, from classical to gospel.

322. **LEARN TO APPRECIATE ABSTRACT ART.** It's a matter of developing your responses to shapes, hues and textures on all levels – mental, emotional and spiritual. By accustomizing yourself to abstraction, you are breaking out of prescriptive categories, and this can only be good for your own creativity.

323. SPEND AN EVENING AT THE BALLET. Romantic ballets, such as Marius Petipa's *Swan Lake* and *Sleeping Beauty* (both of which are set to scores by the Russian composer, Tchaikovsky) are particularly relaxing. You can absorb yourself completely in the spectacle, as groups of dancers weave intricate patterns in synchrony with the music, and soloists inspire wonder with their virtuosity.

324. TAKE TO THE STAGE. As children we make sense of our world through play-acting, but as adults most of us turn our backs on this aspect of creativity. Tap into the wisdom of drama. Enjoy being someone else for an evening. Take a drama class, or join a theatre group or amateur dramatics society. Perform for children, or, if you're political, consider using street theatre to make a statement.

325. **READ A SONNET.** Like the golden section in a painting, there's something intrinsically satisfying about the fourteen-line structure of a sonnet. Relish the words, rhymes and beauty of the form. Shakespeare's sonnets are the obvious place to start. Or, for a mystical flavour, try Rilke's *Sonnets to Orpheus*.

326. **OPEN A BOOK AT RANDOM** and read for a short while. Appreciate the qualities of the prose, the choice of vocabulary, the structuring of ideas or the narration of events. Consider those countries where illiteracy and/or censorship are rife and relish the privilege you're enjoying – to be a reader of a book of your choice.

PLAYTIME

327. **MAKE TIME FOR LAUGHTER** – an instant energizer that stimulates the chakras of the solar plexus and the sacrum. The solar plexus is associated with intimacy and creativity; the sacrum connects us to the energy of the sun, providing the impetus for all our actions.

328. **HAVE A PILLOW FIGHT.** Playfully bashing each other with pillows is a fun way to release tension – both through the physical exertion and the laughter it provokes.

329. **SPINNING IN A CIRCLE** is a popular childhood game that brings us a giddy sense of freedom and release. Find a clear open space, preferably outside on a soft lawn. With your arms outstretched, spin round and round in a circle. When you feel too dizzy to continue, allow yourself to collapse in a heap until the heaving ground comes to a standstill.

330. **SWINGS AND MERRY-GO-ROUNDS** offer us a brief experience of childhood abandon. Not only are they lots of fun, but the rhythmic motion of the swing and the spinning of the roundabout are soothing to both mind and emotions. Riding on a Ferris wheel or chair lift can provide similar experiences. Although the heights involved are greater (and they are therefore probably not suitable for vertigo sufferers), the movements are more gentle. Allow your legs to swing freely. Enjoy the sensation of being suspended in space.

331. **PLAY WITH A YO-YO.** Allow the rhythmic motion of the reel to calm your frayed nerves. With practice, see if you can master some of the fancy moves – it's always fun to surprise people with improbable skills. Alternatively, you may find juggling more appealing. Begin by practising with two balls in order to master the basic "throw, throw, catch, catch" action; then progress to three balls.

332. **GO ON A WORD SAFARI** every day. Whenever you come across a word you can't imagine yourself using, capture it for your personal word zoo. Remember that zoo animals need lots of exercise: use that word at the next opportunity. A large vocabulary gives you more mastery. Go even further and look up a word each day in the dictionary of a foreign language that you can't speak. Sometimes the sound or construction of the foreign word will be pleasing or unexpected – enjoy the fresh perspective this brings to a concept you have referred to many times without thinking.

MAKING THINGS

333. **DO A JIGSAW** – the more pieces the better. The concentration required to complete the jigsaw will take your mind off any troubles you may be experiencing. Choose the subject of the jigsaw to suit your mood. Rural scenes and expanses of water and sky have a subliminally calming effect.

334. **DRAW SOMETHING WITH YOUR LEFT HAND** – or your right hand if you're left-handed. It can be liberating to have slightly less control over the pencil. With a different side of the brain in charge, the results can be surprisingly creative.

335. **WRITE A LIMERICK** – a nonsense poem consisting of five lines, of which the first rhymes with the second and fifth, and the third rhymes with the fourth. Traditionally the first, second and fifth lines consist of eight syllables, the third of five, and the fourth of six. When composing your limerick let your imagination run riot. For example:

"There was an old woman from Leeds,
Who swallowed a packet of seeds,
From out of her nose
Came a beautiful rose
And out of her mouth grew some weeds."

336. **PRACTISE ORIGAMI,** the Japanese art of paper folding, to clear your mind. Allow your creativity to flow through your fingers, producing anything from simple paper hats to more complex shapes, such as birds and animals.

337. **MAKE A CLAY MODEL.** Choose a subject that captures your imagination – perhaps an animal or figure. Don't worry about making the model realistic. Simply enjoy the tactile pleasure of manipulating the cool clay between your hands.

338. **LEARN TO KNIT.** Once you've got the hang of the basic action, you can knit away at speed, allowing the rhythmic clack of the knitting needles to soothe you. Experiment with different wools and patterns. Enjoy the satisfaction that comes with wearing the beautiful products of your work.

OUT AND ABOUT

339. **PLAY POOH-STICKS** when walking across a bridge over a stream or river with friends. This is a game derived from the children's book *Winnie the Pooh*. First, everybody finds a stick or twig that will float. Then, from the upstream side of the bridge, everybody simultaneously drops their sticks into the water, before rushing to the downstream side of the bridge to see whose stick emerges first. Games such as this bring out our innate sense of playfulness, which is often repressed in daily adult life.

340. **TAKE A BAREFOOT STROLL** along a sandy beach. It's soothing to feel the coarse texture of the sand beneath your feet and hear the rhythmic lapping of the waves against the shore. Alternatively, in the early morning, walk barefoot across the dew-soaked grass of a garden, park or field. Bring your awareness to the solid earth beneath your feet and the wet grass as it brushes your ankles.

341. **ATTUNE YOURSELF TO BIRDSONG.** Learning how to identify the songs of different species of bird is one way to cement your harmony with nature. Practise recognizing the birdsong in a park or garden – or even on your way to work! To help you to distinguish between the different songs and calls, you can buy recorded birdsong with helpful identification notes, or learn simply by watching, listening and consulting a bird-watcher's field guide.

342. **SPEND TIME IN A GARDEN.** Nature has been harnessed to wonderful effects all around the world – for example, think of Zen gardens in Japan, or the bulb fields of Holland. Visit such wonders if you get the chance, but bear in mind too that much more modest gardens can be both inspiring and relaxing. Some private gardens may open up to the public on certain days in the summer. But why not borrow a friend's garden for a few hours? – offer some service in return. There are great spaces in every neighbourhood. Try to spend time in some of them.

343. **COLLECT ACORNS** in autumn. Carry one or two in your pocket, giving them an occasional polish. They provide a small reminder of the miracle of life – that something so large grows from something so small and simple.

344. **GO FISHING** – a tranquil, meditative activity in which a catch is secondary to the benefits of stillness and silence.

345. **DO RAIN MAGIC** to conjure up some rain when the land becomes dry.
Perform the ritual outside: pound the earth with your feet to mimic rain; ripple metal sheets to echo thunder; undulate your body like a windblown tree.

346. **HAVE A SNOWBALL FIGHT.** The breathless excitement and sheer fun of a snowball fight provide welcome respite from the housebound days that tend to dominate winter. Tobogganing produces a similar exhilaration.

Evenings

WINDING DOWN

347. **FREE YOUR MUSCLES.** For instant relaxation after a stressful day, tense, then release all the muscle groups in your body, starting with the head and shoulders, and working your way down to the toes. Finish the exercise with ten deep breaths.

348. **BE CREPUSCULAR** – a word meaning "of twilight". Wherever you are, twilight is a beautiful time of day: the hues of the landscape soften and blur; the lights of civilization glow against a background of residual daylight. Simply hang out in the twilight, enjoying the changing light, or go for a crepuscular walk.

349. **CHANGE INTO A LIGHT DRESSING GOWN AND SLIPPERS** at the start of the evening. This can help you to unwind and means you are ready to hop into bed as soon as you feel sleepy.

350. NEVER WASTE A STARRY NIGHT.

On a warm, clear night, well away from city lights, lie down outside on a rug and gaze up at the sky – after a minute or so your eyes will adapt to the dark and thousands of stars will appear. You are a privileged member of a vast cosmos. Allow its purity and peace to fill your own inner space. Buy a star atlas and learn to pick out certain constellations. The sheer vastness of constellations such as Orion, Leo and Taurus is awesome, and once you can identify them, there is something strangely reassuring and intimate about the act of recognition. If you can find order in the vastness of the universe, surely you can overcome earthly anxieties?

351. **TAKE A SEAWEED BATH.** Bring some seaweed (such as bladder-wrack) back from a trip to the beach. Wrap it in muslin and hang it from the hot faucet as it's running so that the nutrients in the seaweed infuse your bathwater. With the smell of the sea in your nostrils, soak away your cares for at least 15 minutes. After your bath, wrap yourself in a soft, warm robe, and drink lots of water. A seaweed bath has the added benefit of leaving your skin feeling smooth and moisturized. For a more concentrated bath, bring about 1lb (50g) of seaweed to the boil in a large pan of water, turn off the heat and infuse for 30 minutes. Strain and add to your bathwater.

LOOKING BACK, LOOKING FORWARD

352. WRITE REVIEWS OF YOUR MOST PLEASURABLE EXPERIENCES. Depending on how frequently you do this, you could survey the experiences of your day, week, month, year, even life so far. What elements in these experiences were responsible for your enjoyment? Consider how you can have more such experiences to bring greater joy into your life.

353. WRITE REVIEWS OF YOUR WORST EXPERIENCES. What are the common elements in these negative experiences? Ask yourself how you can prevent these from recurring in the future.

354. WRITE A "HAVE DONE" LIST. This is a valuable antidote to ever-increasing "to do" lists, which can trigger anxiety and feelings of being overwhelmed. By making a note of each task you've completed, you'll see how productively you've spent your time, and your self-esteem will grow accordingly.

355. CLOSE THE DAY like a file, and archive it. Are there any subtle frustrations or fears from the day hanging like cobwebs in the darkest corners of your mind? If so, sweep them out. Accept that today is now the past, and cannot be changed – all you can do is learn from your experiences. Now is the time for a good night's sleep, a valuable experience in itself.

356. PLAN THREE GOALS (achievable ones!) for tomorrow – perhaps one at work (to clear your desk, for example), one at home (to discuss an issue or concern with your partner), one for your own time (to write to a friend, thanking them for a gift). Limiting your daily goals to three will help you to set more achievable targets, which when completed benefit your self-esteem. Write your goals down, then resolve not to think about them until the following day. Safe in the knowledge that three of tomorrow's jobs are largely taken care of, you can relax.

OFF TO BED

357. **LEARN YOUR NATURAL SLEEP CYCLE,** and follow it whenever you can. To discover how much sleep your body needs, get ready for bed when you're tired but not exhausted. Read until you feel sleepy. Allow yourself to wake naturally. Experiment for three or four nights in succession to work out the optimum number of hours that your body likes to sleep.

358. **DRINK CAMOMILE TEA** before bedtime. Camomile is a calming, soporific herb that will help you to sleep. Add a spoonful of honey to sweeten the infusion if you find it too bitter.

359. **TAKE A DEEP BREATH** of air outside your door before beginning your usual pre-sleep routine. If you have a garden or backyard, stand there for a few minutes if the weather allows. Soak up the sounds, smells and subtle sights of night-time. This is a good way to detach yourself from daytime concerns.

360. **TIDY YOUR BEDROOM** before going to bed. In doing so you are symbolically drawing a line under the business of the day, and you can fall asleep in the knowledge that your immediate environment is well under your control.

361. SELECT YOUR BEDTIME READING CAREFULLY.

Current affairs can re-energize your mind at the wrong time. Restrict yourself to poetry or works of fiction suitable for mulling over as you drift off to sleep.

362. NEVER TAKE WORK TO BED! However tempting

it may be to read a report in bed, this will blur the boundaries between work and rest, making it more difficult for you to switch off from work concerns when it's time for you to sleep.

363. **MAKE PEACE WITH THE WORLD** before you go to sleep with a simple prayer of forgiveness for yourself and anyone else who may have disturbed your equilibrium.

364. **USE IMAGES TO PRIME RESTFUL SLEEP.** Some people can cue pleasant dreams by meditating on a positive subject – a cherished friend, a much-loved landscape, or a masterpiece of art – for a few minutes before they go to bed. Choose a subject that evokes calm. Meditate on it before sleeping, and after waking from nightmares to avoid slipping back into the same bad dream.

365. **TURN OVER YOUR MATTRESS** once a month. This will prevent the mattress from dipping where you regularly lie, ensuring that it remains firm enough to support your back. Invest in a new mattress every ten years, because the material deteriorates by up to 75 per cent in this time.

WATKINS
Sharing Wisdom Since 1893

The story of Watkins began in 1893, when scholar of esotericism John Watkins founded our bookshop, inspired by the lament of his friend and teacher Madame Blavatsky that there was nowhere in London to buy books on mysticism, occultism or metaphysics. That moment marked the birth of Watkins, soon to become the publisher of many of the leading lights of spiritual literature, including Carl Jung, Rudolf Steiner, Alice Bailey and Chögyam Trungpa.

Today, the passion at Watkins Publishing for vigorous questioning is still resolute. Our stimulating and groundbreaking list ranges from ancient traditions and complementary medicine to the latest ideas about personal development, holistic wellbeing and consciousness exploration. We remain at the cutting edge, committed to publishing books that change lives.

DISCOVER MORE AT:

www.watkinspublishing.com

Read our blog

Watch and listen to
our authors in action

Sign up to
our mailing list

We celebrate conscious, passionate, wise and happy living.
Be part of that community by visiting